Read Well, Write Better
リーディングで鍛える英作文

Joan McConnell
武田　修一
山内　圭

photographs
Getty Images
EPA=時事
AEP=時事
iStockphoto
Nancy Lautenbach
Kiyoshi Yamauchi

音声ファイルのダウンロード／ストリーミング

CD マーク表示がある箇所は、音声を弊社 HP より無料でダウンロード／ストリーミングすることができます。トップページのバナーをクリックし、書籍検索してください。書籍詳細ページに音声ダウンロードアイコンがございますのでそちらから自習用音声としてご活用ください。

https://www.seibido.co.jp

Read Well, Write Better

Copyright © 2016 by Joan McConnell, Shuichi Takeda, Kiyoshi Yamauchi

All rights reserved for Japan.
No part of this book may be reproduced in any form
without permission from Seibido Co., Ltd.

PREFACE

Dear Students,

In real life, we use language as a communication tool. We don't think about the four skills – speaking, listening, reading and writing. Instead we use them in various combinations to suit our needs. For instance, when we meet friends or talk on the phone, we both **speak** and **listen**. When we text or email, we both **write** (the message) and **read** (the reply). When we **read** homework assignments, we often **write** some notes. Clearly we need all the four skills to communicate.

The goal of this new textbook is to help you improve both your reading and your writing skills. As the title implies, if you **read well**, then you can certainly **write better**. From experience – personal and professional – I know that this is true.

Each chapter in this textbook begins with a Reading Passage followed by a series of comprehension questions. Next comes the Focus Point, which serves as the link between the reading and the writing sections. It explains the words or phrases that are highlighted in the Reading Passage. The exercises that follow are progressive in difficulty. In this way, you will gradually become comfortable using them.

Before you try the most challenging writing exercises, you can relax as you enjoy the Coffee Break Section. Then you are ready to do the last two exercises. As we say in English, the best is saved for last!

This textbook has 15 chapters. The format is the same for all with the exception of Chapter 15, which includes a grand review of the writing techniques in all the previous chapters. Don't be afraid. By the time you reach Chapter 15, you will discover that you are writing better because you know how to read well.

In real life, as I said before, speakers use the four skills in various combinations to suit their communication needs. You do this in Japanese, so don't be afraid to do the same in English. Believe me, you will be pleased with the results.

Good luck and enjoy,

Dr. Joanie McConnell

本書の使い方

　多くの優良テキストの中から、本書をお選びいただき誠にありがとうございます。
　このテキストを英語学習の良き友として活用いただければ、優れた英文を読むことが、よい英語を書くことに結びつくことを実感しながら英語力を高めていただけるものと確信いたします。練習問題にも様々な工夫を凝らし、皆様の学習効率が高まるよう配慮しました。
　皆様の心の糧となるエッセイで全章を構成いたしましたので、きっとご満足いただけます。
　以下に挙げたねらいや目標を、頭にしっかり入れて学習すれば、学習効果が上がります。

* **本文**
  300 語前後でまとめられた平易な名文です。英文を読む楽しさを味わってください。音読もお勧めします。

* **"MUST-KNOW" collocations and phrases**
  本文中に出てくる、知っておくべき表現やフレーズを取り出し、日本語訳をつけました。英文を書くときにぜひ使ってみましょう。

Ⅰ　**Comprehension Questions**
　本文を読んだ直後に、その内容をどの程度理解できたかをチェックできます。

Ⅱ　**Guided Summary**
　本文の内容が簡潔に要約されています。活用法を自分で考えてみましょう。英文を要約する練習の解答例としても利用できます。

* **Focus Point**
  各章の本文でフォーカスされている文法重要事項について、まとめて説明をしています。既習の文法事項を再確認しましょう。

Ⅲ　**Warming up for Writing**
　(1) では、本文中の文を、単語をくっつける形で表記しています。また、欠落語を適所に補う練習もします。この問題を解くためには、英文構成力が必要です。ライティングのウォーミングアップとして活用してください。
　(2) では、本文中に使われているフレーズを穴埋め形式で解答します。いずれも英文を書く際に使えるようにしておいた方がいいものです。

Ⅳ　**Slash Writing**
　リスニングとライティングを併せた練習問題となっています。英文を聴く際にも、英文構成力が必要であることがわかります。また、聴いた順にそのまま理解する練習にもなります。

Ⅴ　**Word Order**
　並べ替え問題です。Focus Point で説明された文法事項やその他本文中に出てくる重要表現などを、並べ替え問題でマスターできるように練習するものです。全て正解できるようになったら、語群を隠して和文英訳問題としても挑戦してみてください。

Ⅵ　**Finding Errors**
　英文の語法上または語彙上の誤りを正しいものに直し、日本語訳をする問題です。正確な英文を書くための練習です。

Ⅶ　**Full Writing**
　いよいよ、和文英訳問題への挑戦です。Focus Point で学んだ文法事項、本文で出てきた英語表現を正しく使って、英文にできるかを確かめます。これらの問題ができれば、あなたも立派な英語の書き手に一歩近づきます。頑張って挑戦してみましょう。

CONTENTS (FP＝Focus Point)

Chapter 1 Fast Food: Nothing New under the Sun! 6
〈温故知新〉　(FP：why の使い方)

Chapter 2 Famous Dogs 12
〈吾輩は有名な犬である〉　(FP：who, whom の使い方)

Chapter 3 When Was it Invented? 18
〈発明の歴史〉　(FP：when の使い方)

Chapter 4 Never Give Up: An Anti-Bullying Song 24
〈いじめ撲滅ソング〉　(FP：how の使い方)

Chapter 5 The Migration of the Monarch Butterflies 30
〈渡りをする蝶オオカバマダラ〉　(FP：where の使い方)

Chapter 6 New Foods from the New World 36
〈新世界より〉　(FP：what の使い方)

Chapter 7 Foreign Language Study Makes You a Global Citizen 42
〈外国語学習は地球市民へのパスポート〉　(FP：助動詞の使い方)

Chapter 8 Isaac Lufkin: The Armless Football Player 48
〈両腕のないフットボーラー〉　(FP：動名詞と現在分詞の使い方)

Chapter 9 Atlantis, the Lost Empire: Fact or Fiction? 54
〈失われたアトランティス帝国〉　(FP：現在完了形と現在完了進行形の使い方)

Chapter 10 Pope Francis: A New Kind of Pope 60
〈新たな法王誕生〉　(FP：接続詞の使い方)

Chapter 11 The Power of Meditation 66
〈瞑想の力〉　(FP：比較級の使い方)

Chapter 12 Sedona: Harmony with Nature 72
〈自然の彫刻セドナ〉　(FP：仮定法現在の if の使い方)

Chapter 13 Malala: Champion of Education 78
〈教育のために立ち上がった少女マララ〉　(FP：仮定法過去と仮定法過去完了の if の使い方)

Chapter 14 Universities: Past, Present and Future 84
〈大学の移り変わり〉　(FP：挿入句の使い方)

Chapter 15 Lighting up the Future 90
〈未来を照らす〉　(FP：まとめ)

Fast Food: Nothing New under the Sun!

〈温故知新〉

An old saying reminds us that there is nothing new under the sun. In other words, what we "invent" today is something we borrowed from the past, and adapted to our present needs.

Let's take the example of fast food. Contrary to popular belief, it's not a modern invention. You may be surprised to learn that people have been buying ready-cooked meals for centuries.

Why has fast food been so popular throughout history? The answer is simple. Fast food is quick, convenient and cheap. You don't have to go to the (super)market, cook the meal, and wash the dishes. It makes life easier for working parents. In the past, when many people lived in small rooms with no kitchens, they bought food that was already prepared.

There are many varieties of fast food. They reflect the tastes and traditions of the local population. In the Middle East, for example, people eat kebabs. In Japan, they buy bento boxes. In Italy, they enjoy pizza with many different toppings. In Mexico, they like tacos and burritos. These ethnic dishes are no longer local specialties. They are becoming popular all over the world.

Multinational companies such as McDonald's and Burger King have "globalized" the popularity of the hamburger. But to increase sales, they have adapted it to local tastes. Instead of beef, they make burgers of turkey, salmon, shrimp, tofu or vegetables.

Why are traditional hamburgers losing popularity in the US? Many Americans worry about the health risks. Beef is high in cholesterol and saturated fat. This is **why** fast-food chains in the US are now offering healthy alternatives such as sushi, salad and vegan selections.

Fast food keeps borrowing from the past and adapting to the present.

Chapter 1 ◆ Fast Food: Nothing New under the Sun!

"MUST-KNOW" collocations and phrases

1. there is nothing new under the sun 太陽の下に新しきものなし
2. contrary to ～ ～とは反対に
3. don't have to ～ ～しなくてもよい
4. for example 例えば
5. worry about ～ ～のことを心配する
6. such as ～ ～のような

I Comprehension Questions

本文の内容に合っている文にはTを、合っていない文にはFを（　）内に記入しなさい。

1. (　) Many people believe that fast food is a modern invention.
2. (　) In the past, many people bought prepared food because they had no kitchen.
3. (　) Traditional hamburgers are healthy because they are high in cholesterol and saturated fat.

II Guided Summary

次の英文は本文を要約したものです。(1)から(10)の空所に、下の(a)-(j)から適語を選んで記入し文を完成させなさい。

There is nothing new under the sun. What we invent today is something we (1) _____ from the past. For example, fast food is not a modern (2) _____. For centuries, people have been (3) _____ ready-cooked meals. They are quick, (4) _____ and cheap, especially for people with no kitchens or for (5) _____ parents. Many (6) _____ of fast food are becoming popular all over the world. Multinational companies like McDonald's and Burger King have (7) _____ the popularity of the traditional hamburger. But they are also (8) _____ their menus to local tastes and making non-beef burgers. Amcricans (9) _____ that beef burgers are not good for one's health. That is why fast-food chains are offering healthy (10) _____.

[
(a) varieties　　(b) worry　　(c) convenient　　(d) alternatives　　(e) borrowed
(f) globalized　(g) buying　　(h) adapting　　　(i) invention　　　(j) working
]

Focus Point 《why の使い方》

◆ 理由を尋ねる why（疑問詞の why）

疑問詞の why は「何のために、なぜ」(for what purpose) であるのかを尋ねる疑問文で使われます。語順は次のようになります。

① **Why＋動詞＋主語＋（ある場合は）補語**
   Why is fast food popular?（なぜ、ファストフードは人気があるのですか）
② **Why＋助動詞＋主語＋動詞＋（ある場合は）補語**
   Why has fast food been popular?（なぜ、ファストフードはずっと人気があるのですか）

ex 1) **Why** has fast food been so popular throughout history?（本文第3段落）
   平叙文 Fast food has been so popular throughout history. の理由を尋ねる疑問文。

ex 2) **Why** are traditional hamburgers losing popularity in the US?（本文第6段落）
   Traditional hamburgers are losing popularity in the US. の理由を尋ねる疑問文。

◆ 理由を修飾する why（関係副詞の why）

関係副詞の why は、何の理由であるのかを説明する場合に使われます。

ex 3) There are many reasons (**why**) I got angry.（私が腹を立てた理由はたくさんあります）
   関係副詞の why の先行詞は reasons となります。

ex 4) This is **why** fast-food chains in the US are now offering healthy alternatives such as sushi, salad and vegan selections.（本文第6段落）
   This is why ～ で「これが～の理由である」という意味を表します。This is the reason why の先行詞 the reason が省略されたとも、why の中に先行詞が含まれるとも考えられます。

◆ その他の why を用いた表現

その他、why を用いた重要表現に次のようなものがあります。

ex 5) **Why don't you** come to my house tomorrow?（明日、我が家においでよ）
   Why don't you ～ ? で「～しませんか、～した方がいいですよ」などの提案・忠告を表します。ここでは、「あなたは、なぜ明日我が家に来ないのか！」と来ることができない理由を尋ねているのではなく、「なぜ、来ないということがあろうか、そんな理由はない、ぜひ来てください」という提案。

ex 6) **Why**, it's raining!（あらまあ、雨が降ってるよ！）
   why は間投詞としても使われ、「おや、まあ」など驚き・不満などの気持ちを表します。

Chapter 1 ◆ Fast Food: Nothing New under the Sun!

III Warming up for Writing

（1）次の一連の文字群を、適切に切り離し英文を完成しなさい。ただし〈　〉内の単語が欠落しているので適所に補いなさい。

1. Anoldsayingremindsthattherenothingnewunderthesun. 〈us, is〉
   _____

2. Fastfoodkeepsborrowingthepastandadaptingthepresent. 〈from, to〉
   _____

（2）次の日本語に相当する英語表現になるように（　）に適語を書きなさい。

1. 言い換えると
   in (　　　) (　　　)

2. 私たちの現在のニーズ
   our (　　　) needs

3. 一般的に信じられていること
   (　　　) belief

4. 何世紀もの間
   (　　　) centuries

5. 歴史上ずっと
   (　　　) history

6. 皿を洗う
   (　　　) the (　　　)

7. 台所なしの小さな部屋
   (　　　) rooms (　　　) (　　　) kitchens

8. 世界中で
   (　　　) (　　　) the world

IV Slash Writing

日本語を見ながら音声を聴き、英文を書き取りなさい。　🎧 4~6

1. なぜ / ファストフードがそんなに人気がありましたか / 歴史上ずっと
   _____ / _____ fast food _____ so popular / throughout _____ ?

2. あなたは驚くかもしれません / 知って / 人々がずっと買ってきている / 出来合いの食事を / 何世紀もの間
   You may be _____ / to _____ that / people have _____ _____ / _____ meals / for centuries.

3. これが理由です / アメリカ合衆国のファストフードチェーンが / 現在提供している / 健康的な選択肢を / 例えば寿司やサラダや菜食主義者用の品ぞろえなどを
   This is _____ / fast-food _____ in the US / are now _____ / healthy _____ / such as sushi, salad and vegan _____ .

V Word Order

日本語を参考にして下にある語句を並べ替え英文を完成しなさい。

1. 言い換えれば、彼女がこの学校で一番美しい女の子であるということです。
   words, / girl / in / other / the most / she is / beautiful / in this school

   _____

2. 一般的に信じられていることとは反対に、アメリカで伝統的なハンバーガーの人気は落ちている。
   to / contrary / traditional hamburgers / losing / popular belief, / popularity / are / in the US

   _____

3. なぜ野球は歴史上ずっとそんなに人気があったのですか。
   throughout / has / why / history / been / so / baseball / popular / ?

   _____

4. なぜファストフードは仕事をしている親たちの生活を楽にしているのですか。
   easier / life / why / make / does / working parents / fast food / for / ?

   _____

5. これが、英国でフィッシュ・アンド・チップスがそんなに人気がある理由です。
   why / are / so / this / is / fish and chips / popular / in the UK

   _____

6. 彼は、ハンバーガーやフライドポテトなどのファストフードが好きです。
   such / likes / as / fast food / he / French fries / hamburgers / and

   _____

COFFEE BREAK

Genghis Khan's Fast Food
「ジンギス・カンのファストフード」

ジンギス・カンが軍隊を引き連れてアジアを渡った際、兵士たちは食事を作る時間がありませんでした。資料によると、兵士たちは馬の鞍の下に薄切りの生肉を置いて移動したそうです。馬の歩みの動きにより肉がやわらかくなったそうです。彼らは、後でこの「ファストフード」を食べました。この「ファストフード」、どんな味がしたのでしょう？

VI Finding Errors

次の各文には語法または語彙上の誤りが2個所ずつあります。その個所に下線を引き、それを適切な語句に直し（　）内に記入しなさい。また、全文の日本語訳を書きなさい。

1. A old proverb reminds people of there is nothing new under the sun.
   (　　　　　　) (　　　　　　)

2. Why is Shakespeare been such popular throughout history?
   (　　　　　　) (　　　　　　)

3. When he lived in a small room without no kitchen, he bought food what was already cooked.
   (　　　　　　) (　　　　　　)

4. Large companies such as Toyota and Nissan has "globalized" the popular of Japanese cars.
   (　　　　　　) (　　　　　　)

5. This is who they have adapting their menu items to local tastes.
   (　　　　　　) (　　　　　　)

VII Full Writing

次の日本語を英語に直しなさい。

1. そのチームが試合に負けた理由はたくさんあります。

2. あなたは、人々が何世紀にもわたってこの伝統食を食べ続けていると知ったら、驚くでしょう。

3. なぜ、日本で伝統的な台所が人気を失っているのですか。

4. 伝統的なハンバーガーはコレステロールと飽和脂肪が多い。

Famous Dogs

〈吾輩は有名な犬である〉

Some people are famous, others are just ordinary. The same holds true for dogs. **Who** are some of these famous dogs?

Hachiko is certainly at the top of the list of loyal dogs. Although this famous Akita died in 1935, visitors from Japan and abroad still go to Shibuya Station. There they admire his statue, and praise his loyalty.

Some dogs are heroes. Barry, a huge St. Bernard, is perhaps the most famous rescue dog. The monks in Switzerland trained him to save people **who** got lost in the Alps. During his career, he rescued 40 people including a little boy. With the child holding onto his neck, Barry carried him to safety.

Who was the first therapy dog? She was a tiny Yorkshire terrier named Smoky. In 1944, an American soldier rescued her. When he became sick, Smoky went to visit him in the hospital. The soldier's condition improved as soon as he saw her. The doctors were so impressed that they let Smoky visit the other patients. The little dog made them feel happier and less stressed.

For 12 years, Smoky went to visit patients in many hospitals. Thanks to her example, health professionals began to understand the importance of animal therapy. Today dogs, cats, rabbits and even birds are used in animal therapy.

Who is the most famous dog in Hollywood? Most people would agree that it is a beautiful collie named Lassie. She was not a real dog but rather a fictional heroine in many movies. Thanks to her popularity, Lassie earned a "star" on the Hollywood Walk of Fame.

It's fun to learn about famous dogs. Let's not forget, however, the ordinary ones **who** have helped, loved, and protected their owners. In their own way, these dogs are famous.

Chapter 2 ◆ Famous Dogs

"MUST-KNOW" collocations and phrases

1. the top of the list リストのトップ
2. get lost 迷子になる、道に迷う
3. during one's career 〜の現役時代に
4. as soon as 〜 〜するやいなや、〜するとすぐに
5. thanks to 〜 〜のおかげで、〜のため
6. in one's own way 〜の方法で

I Comprehension Questions

本文の内容に合っている文には T を、合っていない文には F を（　）内に記入しなさい。

1. (　) Barry was a huge dog who trained the monks to save people lost in the Alps.
2. (　) Smoky visited the patients when they were happier and less stressed.
3. (　) Lassie is a fictional collie who earned a "star" on the Hollywood Walk of Fame.

II Guided Summary

次の英文は本文を要約したものです。(1) から (10) の空所に、下の (a)-(j) から適語を選んで記入し文を完成させなさい。

There are famous people and also famous dogs. Hachiko is still remembered for his (1) _____ . Barry is the famous St. Bernard who (2) _____ 40 people who got lost in the Alps. Smoky was the first (3) _____ dog. An American (4) _____ rescued this tiny Yorkshire terrier. When he became sick, she (5) _____ him in the hospital. His condition (6) _____ so the doctors let her visit the other patients. Thanks to Smoky, health (7) _____ use (8) _____ therapy. Lassie is probably the most famous dog in Hollywood. She was not a real dog but rather a (9) _____ character in many movies. Thanks to her (10) _____ , Lassie earned a "star" on the Hollywood Walk of Fame.

[
(a) animal　　(b) visited　　(c) fictional　　(d) therapy　　(e) loyalty
(f) popularity　(g) professionals　(h) soldier　(i) improved　(j) saved
]

Focus Point 《who/whom の使い方》

◆ 「誰か」を尋ねる who（疑問詞の who）

疑問詞の who は疑問文で主語となる代名詞で、次のように使います。

① **Who** likes dogs?（犬が好きなのは誰ですか）
　応答例１：Hidesaburo likes dogs.（英三郎が犬が好きです）
　応答例２：Hidesaburo (does).（英三郎〈です〉）

② **Who** has been abroad?（誰が外国に行ったことがありますか）
　応答例１：Yukichi and Manjiro have been abroad.
　　　　　（諭吉と万次郎が外国に行ったことがあります）
　応答例２：Yukichi and Manjiro (have).（諭吉と万次郎〈があります〉）

ex 1) **Who** are some of these famous dogs?（本文第１段落）
ex 2) **Who** was the first therapy dog?（本文第４段落）
ex 3) **Who** is the most famous dog in Hollywood?（本文第６段落）
　　　who は人間だけでなく、動物などにも使われます。

◆ 「どんな人なのか」を説明する who（関係代名詞の who）

人がどのような人であるかを説明する時に関係代名詞の who が使われます。

ex 4) The monks in Switzerland trained him to save people **who** got lost in the Alps.（本文第３段落）
　　　「アルプスで迷った」(who got lost in the Alps) が「人々」(people) を修飾しています。
　　　→「アルプスで迷った人々」

ex 5) Let's not forget, however, the ordinary ones **who** have helped, loved, and protected their owners.（本文第７段落）
　　　「飼い主を助けたり、愛したり、守ったりした」(who have helped, loved, and protected their owners) が「普通の者たち（犬たち）」(the ordinary ones) を修飾しています。

◆ 「誰に」を尋ねる whom（疑問詞 whom）

疑問詞 whom は目的格で動詞または前置詞の目的語として使われます。whom は文語的で、会話では、あまり用いられません。逆に英文を書く際に使うことができたら格調高い英文となります。

① **動詞の目的語として使用**
　Whom did you see at the party?（あなたはパーティで誰に会ったのですか）
　応答例１：I saw Anna and Elsa.（私はアナとエルサに会いました）
　応答例２：Anna and Elsa.（アナとエルサ〈です〉）

② **前置詞の目的語として使用**
　To whom did you give the key?（あなたは誰に鍵を渡したのですか）
　応答例１：I gave the key to my son.（私の息子に渡しました）
　応答例２：My son.（私の息子〈です〉）

III Warming up for Writing

（1）次の一連の文字群を、適切に切り離し英文を完成しなさい。ただし〈　〉内の単語が欠落しているので適所に補いなさい。

1. WiththechildholdinghisneckBarrycarriedhimsafety. 〈onto, to〉

_____

2. ThemonksinSwitzerlandtrainedhimsavepeoplegotlostintheAlps. 〈to, who〉

_____

（2）次の日本語に相当する英語表現になるように（　）に適語を書きなさい。

1. ～にも当てはまる
   the same (　　　) (　　　) for ～
2. リストのトップ
   the (　　　) (　　　) the list
3. 日本からの訪問者たち
   (　　　) (　　　) Japan
4. 彼の忠誠心をたたえる
   (　　　) his (　　　)
5. 一人の幼い少年も含めて 40 人
   40 people (　　　) a little boy
6. 彼を病院に見舞う
   go to (　　　) him in the (　　　)
7. 医療職者たち
   health (　　　)
8. ラッシーという名のコリー犬
   a collie (　　　) Lassie

IV Slash Writing

日本語を見ながら音声を聴き、英文を書き取りなさい。　🎧 9~11

1. この有名な秋田犬は 1935 年に死にましたが / 日本や外国からの訪問者たちは / 今でも行きます / 渋谷駅に

   Although this _____ Akita died in 1935, /
   visitors _____ Japan and _____ / _____ go /
   _____ Shibuya Station.

2. スイスの修道士たちは / 彼を訓練した / 人々を助けるために / アルプスで道に迷った

   The _____ in Switzerland / _____ him / to _____ people /
   who _____ _____ in the Alps.

3. 忘れないようにしよう / しかしながら / 普通のものたちを / 自分たちの飼い主を助け、愛し、守った

   Let's not _____, / _____, / the _____ ones /
   who have _____, loved, and _____ their owners.

V Word Order

日本語を参考にして下にある語句を並べ替え英文を完成しなさい。

1. 犬には有名なものもいれば、単に普通のものもいる。
   dogs / are / are / just / some / others / famous / ordinary

   _____

2. イチロー選手は、確かに好打者のリストのトップである。
   Ichiro / is / at the top / of / of / good batters / certainly / the list

   _____

3. この大学で一番有名な教授は誰ですか。
   the / is / in / who / famous / most/ professor / this university / ?

   _____

4. 上野英三郎博士は、ハチ公を飼っていた教授でした。
   professor / Dr. Hidesaburo Ueno / Hachiko / the / owned / was / who

   _____

5. 彼が病気になった時、彼のガールフレンドが病院の彼を見舞いに行った。
   him / he became sick, / in the hospital / when / his girlfriend / to / went / visit

   _____

6. フローレンス・ナイチンゲールのおかげで医療職者たちは、統計学の重要性を理解し始めた。
   thanks to / the importance / health / began to understand / Florence Nightingale, / professionals / of / statistics

   _____

The Most Famous Cartoon Dog
「漫画で一番有名な犬」

漫画で一番有名な犬は何でしょうか。それは、おそらくスヌーピーでしょう。この愛すべき犬は、1950年10月4日に初めて登場しました。スヌーピーは、有名な漫画家チャールズ・シュルツによって生み出されました。彼は今や60歳を超えていますが、人々は今でも彼を愛しています。

VI Finding Errors

次の各文には語法または語彙上の誤りが2個所ずつあります。その個所に下線を引き、それを適切な語句に直し(　)内に記入しなさい。また、全文の日本語訳を書きなさい。

1. Mickey are perhaps the more well-known animated mouse.
　　　　　　　　　　　　　　　　　(　　　　　　) (　　　　　　)
　_____

2. While his career, he saved 40 people included a little boy.
　　　　　　　　　　　　　　　　　(　　　　　　) (　　　　　　)
　_____

3. The condition of the patients which saw the therapy dog improvemented.
　　　　　　　　　　　　　　　　　(　　　　　　) (　　　　　　)
　_____

4. The cat made them feeling happier and less stress.
　　　　　　　　　　　　　　　　　(　　　　　　) (　　　　　　)
　_____

5. Most peoples would agree who the biggest famous dog in the movies is.
　　　　　　　　　　　　　　　　　(　　　　　　) (　　　　　　)
　_____

VII Full Writing

次の日本語を英語に直しなさい。

1. バリーは、確かにレスキュー犬のリストのトップにいます。
　_____

2. 1944年に誰がその犬を救ったのですか。
　_____

3. 10年間、ハチ公は彼の飼い主に会うために渋谷駅に行きました。
　_____

4. ジョン・スタインベック（John Steinbeck）は『エデンの東』(*East of Eden*) を書いたアメリカ人作家です。
　_____

When Was it Invented?

〈発明の歴史〉

Today we take for granted many things such as eyeglasses, cell phones and common medicines. But they have not always been available.

Let's start with the telephone. **When** was it invented?

In 1876, Alexander Graham Bell created a machine for "long distance" talking. He called it the telephone. Today this technology is more sophisticated. Now with our smartphones, we can email, text, pay bills, make reservations, watch movies and much more.

When did people start wearing eyeglasses? The first were probably invented in Italy around the middle of the 13th century. Since then, there have been many innovations – bifocals, trifocals, sunglasses as well as progressive and photochromic lenses.

If you have a headache, fever or muscle pain, this is the time **when** you may take an aspirin for relief. Do you know **when** this drug was created? In 1897, the chemist Felix Hoffmann prepared aspirin for Bayer, the famous German pharmaceutical company. Today doctors often recommend low doses of aspirin to reduce the risk of heart attacks.

One hundred years ago, there were no adhesive bandages to protect an open wound. **When** were they invented? In 1920, Earle Dickson attached a piece of cotton gauze to an adhesive strip so that the protective cover would not move. His boss, one of the founders of the pharmaceutical company named Johnson and Johnson, was impressed. In 1924, the company started mass production of Band-Aids, its trademark product.

If you have a bacterial infection, your doctor may prescribe an antibiotic. You are lucky because in the past, there was no cure.

When did antibiotics enter medical history? In 1928, a Scottish scientist named Alexander Fleming discovered penicillin, the first antibiotic. It has saved the lives of millions of people.

When you want to learn, don't be afraid to ask questions.

Chapter 3 ◆ When Was it Invented?

"MUST-KNOW" collocations and phrases

1. take for granted 当たり前と思う
2. start with ~ ~で始める
3. one of the ~ ~のうちの一人（一つ）
4. in the past 過去に
5. millions of ~ 何百万もの~
6. don't be afraid to ~ ~することをおそれない、おそれず~する

I Comprehension Questions

本文の内容に合っている文にはTを、合っていない文にはFを（　）内に記入しなさい。

1. (　) Alexander Graham Bell's telephone is a machine for long-distance talking.
2. (　) Felix Hoffmann, the chemist who prepared aspirin, recommended low doses of this drug to reduce the risk of heart attacks.
3. (　) The first antibiotic was penicillin, discovered by a Scottish scientist named Alexander Fleming.

II Guided Summary

次の英文は本文を要約したものです。(1) から (10) の空所に、下の (a)-(j) から適語を選んで記入し文を完成させなさい。

Today we take for (1) _____ many things such as eyeglasses, cell phones and common medicines. When were they (2) _____? In 1876, Alexander Graham Bell created a long-distance talking machine called the (3) _____. With today's smartphones, we can text, email, pay bills and much more. Eyeglasses were invented in Italy around the middle of the 13th century. Thanks to modern (4) _____, we now have bifocals, trifocals as well as progressive and photochromic lenses. In 1897, the chemist Felix Hoffmann synthesized aspirin. This drug (5) _____ headaches, fever and muscle pain, and may also (6) _____ the risk of heart attacks. (7) _____ bandages were invented in 1920 by Earle Dickson. Since 1924, the (8) _____ company Johnson and Johnson has mass-produced their (9) _____ brand Band-Aids. In 1928, the Scottish scientist Alexander Fleming (10) _____ penicillin, the first antibiotic.

(a) reduce (b) trademark (c) technology (d) discovered
(e) granted (f) adhesive (g) invented (h) relieves
(i) pharmaceutical (j) telephone

《when の使い方》

◆ 時を尋ねる when (疑問詞の when)

時を尋ねる疑問文では、疑問詞の when を使います。語順は直接疑問文では、when を文頭に置き、以降は疑問文の語順となり、間接疑問文では、when の後ろは平叙文の語順となります。

[直接疑問文]
When is she going shopping?（彼女はいつ買い物に行きますか）
応答例１：She is going shopping tomorrow.（彼女は明日買い物に行きます）
応答例２：Tomorrow.（明日です）

ex 1) **When** did people start wearing eyeglasses?（本文第４段落）
ex 2) **When** did antibiotics enter medical history?（本文第８段落）
ex 3) **When** was it [the telephone] invented?（本文第２段落）
ex 4) **When** were they [adhesive bandages] invented?（本文第６段落）

[間接疑問文]
ex 5) Do you know **when** this drug was created?（本文第５段落）
 応答例：Yes I/we do. This drug was created in 1897.
 （はい、知っています。この薬は 1897 年に創り出されました）
 ただし、know の代わりに think が使われるときは、次のようになり語順に注意する必要があります。
 When do you think this drug was created?（あなたは、いつこの薬が創り出されたと思いますか）

◆ 「〜した（する）時に」を表す when (接続詞の when)

時を表す接続詞の代表格が when です。「〜した（する）時に」などの意味を表します。
When I was a student, I lived in a very old apartment house in Yokohama.（私が学生だった時には、横浜のとても古いアパートに住んでいました）
過去のある時を表す以外にも、「〜する時（にはいつでも）」と一般的な時を表すこともあります。

ex 6) **When** you want to learn, don't be afraid to ask questions.（本文第９段落）
 ここでの when が導く節は、「あなたが学びたいと思う時には」という意味。

◆ 時を説明する when (関係副詞の when)

関係副詞の when は、その時がどの様な時かを説明する形容詞節を結びつける働きをします。この場合の関係副詞の when は on[at, in] which と置き換え可能です。

ex 7) If you have a headache, fever or muscle pain, this is the time **when** you may take an aspirin for relief.（本文第５段落）
 the time がどんな時かを when you may take an aspirin for relief が修飾しています。

III Warming up for Writing

（1）次の一連の文字群を、適切に切り離し英文を完成しなさい。ただし〈　〉内の単語が欠落しているので適所に補いなさい。

1. Ifyouaheadachefeverormusclepainthisisthetimewhenyoumaytakeanaspirinrelief.
〈have, for〉

_____

2. Todaydoctorsoftenrecommendlowdosesofaspirinreducetheriskheartattacks.
〈to, of〉

_____

（2）次の日本語に相当する英語表現になるように（　）に適語を書きなさい。

1. 当たり前に思う
   take (　　　) (　　　)
2. 携帯電話
   (　　　) phone(s)
3. より洗練された
   more (　　　)
4. 薬品会社
   (　　　) company
5. 絆創膏（ばんそうこう）
   adhesive (　　　)
6. 一切れの綿ガーゼ
   a (　　　) of cotton (　　　)
7. 創始者の一人
   (　　　) of the (　　　)
8. 抗生物質を処方する
   (　　　) an (　　　)

IV Slash Writing

日本語を見ながら音声を聴き、英文を書き取りなさい。　🎧 14~16

1. 現在ではスマホで / 私達は電子メールの送信ができる / 携帯メールをしたり / 料金を支払ったり / 予約をしたり / 映画を見たり / などなども
   Now _____ our smartphones, / we can email, / _____, / pay bills, / make _____, / _____ movies / and much _____.

2. もしあなたに頭痛がある場合 / 発熱や筋肉痛 / これがその時です / あなたがアスピリンを飲む / 緩和のために
   If you have a _____, / fever or _____ pain, / this is the _____ / when you may take an _____ / for _____.

3. あなたが学びたい時には、/ こわがらないで / 質問をすることを
   When you want to _____, / don't be _____ / to ask _____.

V Word Order

日本語を参考にして下にある語句を並べ替え英文を完成しなさい。

1. 今日私たちは、アスピリンや抗生物質や絆創膏などの多くの物を当たり前のことと考えています。
   we / today / for granted / take / such as / aspirin, / many things / antibiotics and adhesive bandages

   _____

2. あなたの妹はいつコンタクトレンズを着用し始めたのですか。
   start / when / wearing / your / lenses / did / sister / contact / ?

   _____

3. 彼女は、勝ったチームのメンバーの一人でした。
   members / of / winning team / she / the / the / one of / was

   _____

4. あなたは、この建物がいつ建てられたのか知っていますか。
   when / built / know / was / do / you / this / building / ?

   _____

5. 何百万人もの命が抗生物質によって救われています。
   with antibiotics / the / millions of / have / saved / lives of / people / been

   _____

6. パーティに出席したら、おそれずに知らない人に話しかけましょう。
   when / attend / you / speak to / a party, / don't / a stranger / be afraid to

   _____

The First Olympic Games
「最初のオリンピック」

最初のオリンピックは、古代ギリシャの聖なる地オリンピアで紀元前776年に行なわれました。この習慣は、約1000年続きましたが、やがて忘れられました。フランスのピエール・デ・クーベルタン男爵の努力のおかげで、第1回近代オリンピックが1896年ギリシャのアテネで開かれました。

VI Finding Errors

次の各文には語法または語彙上の誤りが2個所ずつあります。その個所に下線を引き、それを適切な語句に直し（　）内に記入しなさい。また、全文の日本語訳を書きなさい。

1. Today people take in granted many things such for smartphones and electronic money.
   　　　　　　　　　　　　　　　　　　（　　　　　　　）（　　　　　　　）
   _____

2. When did he start wore eyeglass?
   　　　　　　　　　　　　　　　　　　（　　　　　　　）（　　　　　　　）
   _____

3. Do you think when this machine were created?
   　　　　　　　　　　　　　　　　　　（　　　　　　　）（　　　　　　　）
   _____

4. In 1876, a scientist naming Alexander Graham Bell invents the telephone.
   　　　　　　　　　　　　　　　　　　（　　　　　　　）（　　　　　　　）
   _____

5. This medicine was saved the life of millions of people.
   　　　　　　　　　　　　　　　　　　（　　　　　　　）（　　　　　　　）
   _____

VII Full Writing

次の日本語を英語に直しなさい。

1. 今日私たちは、鉄道や自動車や飛行機などの多くの交通機関を当たり前のことと考えています。
   _____

2. 最初のスマホはいつ創り出されましたか。
   _____

3. 人々はいつからハンバーガーを食べ始めたのですか。
   _____

4. もしあなたが頭痛がすれば、あなたの医師はアスピリンを処方するかもしれません。
   _____

Never Give Up: An Anti-Bullying Song

〈いじめ撲滅ソング〉

    Today bullying is one of the most serious, non-academic problems in schools around the world. Unfortunately bullies attack their victims both at school and on social media. Cyberbullying is especially dangerous because it can ruin the reputation of young people, and also destroy their self-esteem. In some unfortunate cases, the victims have even committed suicide.

    How can we put an end to bullying? Parents and teachers are looking for solutions. Politicians, religious leaders and celebrities are speaking out about this problem. The media are doing special reports. Despite all these efforts, there are still no solutions to this problem.

    Peter Yarrow, a famous American folksinger, has an interesting suggestion. He believes that music is a powerful way to fight bullying. In his opinion, a song "speaks" to people because it uses both rhythm and words to send a message.

    Yarrow was inspired by a poem written by the Dalai Lama. The great religious leader explained **how** we can eliminate bullying. Here is the Dalai Lama's advice.

    First we must learn **how to** love and forgive ourselves. Once we are at peace with ourselves, we are ready to love and forgive others, even those who have harmed or bullied us. This is the way to promote harmony among individuals and even nations.

    According to the Dalai Lama, we must "Never Give Up" in our struggle to stop bullying. Yarrow uses these three words as the title of his anti-bullying song released in late 2013. The lyrics remind us that the struggle to stop bullying is not easy. It takes time, energy and compassion.

    "Never Give Up" is more than a song. It is a beautiful reminder of **how** the "war" against bullying can be won. With love and forgiveness, people can live together in peace and harmony.

Chapter 4 ◆ Never Give Up: An Anti-Bullying Song

"MUST-KNOW" collocations and phrases

1. commit suicide　自殺する、自死する
2. put an end to ～　～を終わりにする
3. in one's opinion　～の考えでは
4. be ready to ～　～する準備ができている
5. according to ～　～によると
6. live together in peace and harmony　平和に共生する

I Comprehension Questions

本文の内容に合っている文にはTを、合っていない文にはFを（　）内に記入しなさい。

1. (　) Bullying is the only serious problem in schools around the world.
2. (　) When we love and forgive others, we are ready to love and forgive ourselves.
3. (　) The song "Never Give Up" reminds us that it takes time, energy and compassion to win the "war" against bullying.

II Guided Summary

次の英文は本文を要約したものです。(1) から (10) の空所に、下の (a)-(j) から適語を選んで記入し文を完成させなさい。　CD 18

Today bullying is a (1) _____ problem in schools. Cyberbullying can (2) _____ young people's reputations and (3) _____. Some victims commit (4) _____. Unfortunately nobody has (5) _____ to this problem. The American folksinger Peter Yarrow believes in the power of music because the (6) _____ and words of a song send a message. Yarrow was (7) _____ by a poem in which the Dalai Lama (8) _____ how to stop bullying. We must first love and forgive ourselves, and then we can love and forgive others, even enemies. This (9) _____ is not easy, but the Dalai Lama tells us "Never Give Up." Yarrow uses these three words as the (10) _____ of his anti-bullying song.

[
(a) explains　(b) suicide　(c) title　(d) self-esteem　(e) serious
(f) lesson　(g) inspired　(h) solutions　(i) ruin　(j) rhythm
]

Focus Point 《how の使い方》

◆ **方法を尋ねる how（疑問詞の how）**

疑問詞の how は「どのように」を意味し、方法を尋ねる時に使います。直接疑問文にも間接疑問文にも使われます。

ex 1) **How** can we put an end to bullying?（本文第2段落）
いじめの終わらせ方を尋ねる直接疑問文。「私たちにはいじめをどのように終わらせることができるかわからない」という間接疑問文は、We don't know **how** we can put an end to bullying. となります。how 以下が we can と平叙文の語順になっています。

ex 2) The great religious leader explained **how** we can eliminate bullying.（本文第4段落）
how we can eliminate bullying で「どのようにいじめを排除できるか」という意味。動詞 explain(ed) の直接目的語になっています。

ex 3) It is a beautiful reminder of **how** the "war" against bullying can be won.（本文第7段落）
how 節が前置詞 of の目的語となっています。

◆ **「how ＋ to 不定詞」**

疑問詞の how に to 不定詞をつけて「〜の仕方、〜する方法」などの意味を表します。

ex 4) First we must learn **how to** love and forgive ourselves.（本文第5段落）
how to love and forgive と how to の後に love と forgive という2つの動詞があります。

◆ **感嘆文を作る how（感嘆詞の how）**

「何て〜だろう」と感嘆の気持ちを表す時に how を使って表現することができます。名詞句が中心となる what を使った感嘆文と違い、how を使った感嘆文は、形容詞または副詞が注目されています。

How beautiful this flower is!（この花はなんて美しいのでしょう）

◆ **程度を尋ねる how**

下記のように、形容詞または副詞と結びついて、程度を尋ねる疑問文を作ります。
① **数量を尋ねる how many**：**How many** students are there in this room?
（この部屋には何人の学生がいますか）
② **年齢を尋ねる how old**：**How old** is the professor?（その教授は何歳ですか）
③ **値段を尋ねる how much**：**How much** is this textbook?（この教科書はいくらですか）
④ **頻度を尋ねる how often**：**How often** do you water the flowers?
（どのくらいの頻度で花に水やりをしますか）

III Warming up for Writing

（1）次の一連の文字群を、適切に切り離し英文を完成しなさい。ただし〈　〉内の単語が欠落しているので適所に補いなさい。

1. Unfortunatelybulliesattacktheirvictimsbothschoolandsocialmedia. 〈at, on〉
   _____

2. Firstwemustlearnloveandforgiveourselves. 〈how, to〉
   _____

（2）次の日本語に相当する英語表現になるように（　）に適語を書きなさい。

1. この問題について発言する
   speak (　　　) (　　　) this problem

2. これらの努力にも関わらず
   (　　　) all these efforts

3. 詩によって着想を得る
   be (　　　) by a poem

4. 自分自身に安らぎを得る
   be at (　　　) (　　　) oneself

5. 私たちに被害を与えたりいじめたりした人たち
   (　　　) who have harmed or (　　　) us

6. 個人間の協調
   harmony (　　　) individuals

7. ダライラマによると
   (　　　) to (　　　) Dalai Lama

8. 決してあきらめるな
   (　　　) give up

IV Slash Writing

日本語を見ながら音声を聴き、英文を書き取りなさい。　CD 19~21

1. 今日 / いじめは最も深刻な / 学校での学業以外の問題です / 世界中で
   Today / bullying is _____ of the most _____ , / non-academic _____ in _____ / _____ the world.

2. どのようにして / 終わりにできるのか / いじめを
   _____ / can we _____ an _____ / to _____ ?

3. それは美しく思い出させてくれるものです / どのようにしていじめに対する「戦争」に / 勝つことができるかを
   It is a beautiful _____ / of _____ the "war" against bullying / can be _____ .

V Word Order

日本語を参考にして下にある語句を並べ替え英文を完成しなさい。

1. 政治家たち、宗教的指導者たち、そして有名人たちは、差別のなくし方はわかりません。
   and celebrities / don't know / politicians, / how / to / religious leaders / eliminate / discrimination

   _____

2. その偉大な政治家は、その国の赤字の減らし方を説明しました。
   explained / reduce / the / how / politician / great / to / the country's deficit

   _____

3. これが、個人間、そしてさらに国家間の友情を促進する方法です。
   promote / even nations / this is / the way / and / to / among individuals / friendship

   _____

4. ヤロウ氏は、2013年暮れにリリースした彼のいじめ撲滅の歌の題名として「決してあきらめるな」を使います。
   his anti-bullying song / Yarrow / as the title / "Never Give Up" / of / uses / in late 2013 / released

   _____

5. その詩は、偏見をなくす戦いが簡単なものではないことを私たちに思い起こさせてくれます。
   that / reminds us / is not easy / prejudice / the poem / to / the struggle / stop

   _____

6. 愛情と寛容の心で、人々は共生の仕方を学ぶことができるのです。
   can / people / live together / with love / how / learn / and forgiveness, / to

   _____

The Golden Rule
「黄金律」

黄金律とは、私たちがふるまうべき方法についての万人共通の判断基準です。それは、自分が接してもらいたいように他人に接しなさいということを私たちに教えてくれます。もし、世界中の人々が、この黄金律に従えば、いじめなんてなくなるでしょう。

VI Finding Errors

次の各文には語法または語彙上の誤りが2個所ずつあります。その個所に下線を引き、それを適切な語句に直し（　）内に記入しなさい。また、全文の日本語訳を書きなさい。

1. Now bullying is one of the most serious, non-academic problem in schools around the worlds.
   (　　　　　　　) (　　　　　　　)

2. How can they put on end to bully?
   (　　　　　　　) (　　　　　　　)

3. Inspite all the efforts, there are still any solutions to this problem.
   (　　　　　　　) (　　　　　　　)

4. Many people have inspired by poems wrote by Walt Whitman.
   (　　　　　　　) (　　　　　　　)

5. We have to learn way to love and forgive ourself.
   (　　　　　　　) (　　　　　　　)

VII Full Writing

次の日本語を英語に直しなさい。

1. 不幸な場合は、戦争に行った人たちの中には自殺をする人がいます。

2. どうしたら私たちはテロを終わらせることができるのでしょうか。

3. 彼の考えでは、これが個人間、そしてさらに国家間の調和を促進する方法です。

4. あなたはどれくらいの頻度でコンビニに行きますか。

The Migration of the Monarch Butterflies

〈渡りをする蝶オオカバマダラ〉

　　When I was a little girl, I loved to chase butterflies. They were so beautiful and graceful that I wanted to be near them. My favorite was the gorgeous orange and black monarch butterfly.

　　Every year in September and early October, these butterflies disappeared. One day I asked my mother **where** they had gone. She told me that the butterflies were following the sun.

　　Years later, I discovered that my mother was right. I also discovered **where** the monarch butterflies go. Every fall, they leave their "summer" home in the north, and migrate to California and Mexico **where** the weather is warm. Guided by the sun, they fly during the day, and rest at night. It takes them almost two months to reach their "winter" home.

　　This migration is truly a miracle of nature. A monarch butterfly weighs less than half a gram, and has a wingspan of approximately 10 centimeters. Yet these fragile creatures have the strength to fly thousands of miles. Their survival depends on spending the winter in a warm climate.

　　Where can you see these special butterflies? The best place is the Monarch Butterfly Biosphere Reserve. This World Heritage Site is located about 100 kilometers west of Mexico City. Every winter, millions of monarch butterflies come to this peaceful forest. Between November and March, you can see one of nature's amazing spectacles.

　　At night, the monarch butterflies sleep on the tree branches, but when the sun rises, they wake up. Suddenly the forest is filled with millions of butterflies. Some cluster in large groups, while others prefer to fly in pairs, like lovers. But all of them follow the sun as it filters through the trees.

　　My mother was right about **where** monarch butterflies go. They follow the sun.

Chapter 5 ◆ The Migration of the Monarch Butterflies

"MUST-KNOW" collocations and phrases

1. a miracle of nature　自然の奇跡
2. depend on ～　～による
3. in a warm climate　暖かい気候で
4. is located about 100 kilometers west of ～
　～から西に約 100 キロに位置する
5. be filled with ～　～でいっぱいである
6. cluster in large groups　大きいいくつかの群れとなる

I Comprehension Questions

本文の内容に合っている文には T を、合っていない文には F を (　) 内に記入しなさい。

1. (　) Every fall, the monarch butterflies migrate to California and Mexico where the weather is warm.
2. (　) These tiny, fragile butterflies fly thousands of miles at night.
3. (　) The author learned that butterflies follow the sun.

II Guided Summary

次の英文は本文を要約したものです。(1) から (10) の空所に、下の (a)-(j) から適語を選んで記入し文を完成させなさい。

I have always loved (1) ＿＿＿＿, especially the gorgeous orange and black monarch. Every year in September and early October, they leave their (2) ＿＿＿＿ home in the north and (3) ＿＿＿＿ to California and Mexico where the weather is warm. They are (4) ＿＿＿＿ by the sun. They fly during the day and (5) ＿＿＿＿ at night. These tiny, fragile creatures can fly (6) ＿＿＿＿ of miles. The Monarch Butterfly Biosphere Reserve in Mexico is the best place to (7) ＿＿＿＿ an amazing (8) ＿＿＿＿ of nature. When the sun rises, you will see (9) ＿＿＿＿ of butterflies. It's true that they (10) ＿＿＿＿ the sun.

(a) guided　(b) experience　(c) follow　(d) butterflies　(e) spectacle
(f) rest　(g) thousands　(h) summer　(i) millions　(j) migrate

《where の使い方》

◆ 場所を尋ねる where（疑問詞の where）

疑問詞の where は、場所を尋ねる疑問文で使われます。直接疑問文では、where の後は疑問文の語順となり、間接疑問文では平叙文の語順となります。

[直接疑問文]
ex 1) **Where** can you see these special butterflies?（本文第5段落）
　　　応答例1：We can see them [these special butterflies] in California and Mexico.
　　　　　　（私たちはそれら[特別な蝶]をカリフォルニアとメキシコで見ることができます）
　　　応答例2：In California and Mexico.（カリフォルニアとメキシコです）

[間接疑問文]
ex 2) One day I asked my mother **where** they had gone.（本文第2段落）
　　　間接疑問文の場合は、where they had gone の語順となり、動詞 asked の直接目的語になっています。

ex 3) I also discovered **where** the monarch butterflies go.（本文第3段落）
　　　where the butterflies go が動詞 discovered の直接目的語になっています。

ex 4) My mother was right about **where** monarch butterflies go.（本文第7段落）
　　　where が導く間接疑問文は前置詞 about の目的語になっています。

◆ 場所を説明する where（関係副詞の where）

関係副詞の where は、その場所がどんな場所かを説明する形容詞句を結びつける働きをします。この場合の where は in[at, on] which と置き換えが可能です。

ex 5) Every fall, they leave their "summer" home in the north, and migrate to California and Mexico **where** the weather is warm.（本文第3段落）
　　　where the weather is warm（気候が暖かい）の関係副詞節は場所である California and Mexico（カリフォルニア及びメキシコ）を修飾しています。

◆ その他の where の用法

where には、「～するところはどこにも」という接続詞的な使い方もあります。
Where there is a will, there is a way.（意志あるところに道あり、「精神一到何事か成らざらん」）
Where there is smoke, there is fire.（煙のあるところに火あり、「火のないところに煙は立たず」）

Chapter 5 ◆ The Migration of the Monarch Butterflies

III Warming up for Writing

（1）次の一連の文字群を、適切に切り離し英文を完成しなさい。ただし〈　〉内の単語が欠落しているので適所に補いなさい。

1. Theywerebeautifulandgracefullwantedtobenearthem.〈so, that〉

_____

2. OnedayIaskedmymothertheygone.〈where, had〉

_____

（2）次の日本語に相当する英語表現になるように（　）に適語を書きなさい。

1. オオカバマダラ蝶
   (　　　) butterflies
2. 毎年９月に
   (　　　) year (　　　) September
3. 太陽を追いかける
   (　　　)(　　　) sun
4. 何年か後
   (　　　) later
5. ～に渡りをする、～に移動〔住〕する
   (　　　) to ～
6. 日中
   (　　　) the day
7. ～未満
   (　　　) than ～
8. 世界遺産の場所
   (　　　)(　　　) Site

IV Slash Writing

日本語を見ながら音声を聴き、英文を書き取りなさい。　🎧 24~26

1. それらはとても美しく優雅で / 私はしたかった / それらのそばにいることを
   They were so _____ and _____ / that I _____ to / be _____ them.

2. 毎年秋に / それらは北の「夏の」すみかを離れ / そしてカリフォルニアやメキシコに渡ります / そこでは気候が暖かい
   Every _____, / they _____ their "summer" home in the north, / and _____ to California and Mexico / where the _____ is _____.

3. 私の母は正しかった / ところ（場所）に関して / オオカバマダラ蝶が行く
   My mother was _____ / about _____ / monarch _____ _____.

V Word Order

日本語を参考にして下にある語句を並べ替え英文を完成しなさい。

1. 太陽に導かれ、ツバメたちは、日中は飛び、夜間は休息します。
   by the sun, / during the day, / at night / and / fly / the swallows / rest / guided

2. 蝶たちが気候の暖かいメキシコに到着するのには、2か月かかります。
   it takes / is warm / where / the butterflies / two months / to reach Mexico / the weather

3. これらの美しくて強い蝶をどこで見ることができるのでしょうか。
   can / beautiful / where / see / butterflies / you / these / and strong / ?

4. しかしながら、これらのきれいな生き物たちは、何千マイルをも飛ぶ強さを持っています。
   fly / these beautiful creatures / to / thousands of miles / the strength / have / yet

5. 毎冬、何百万匹ものオオカバマダラ蝶が、この静かな森にやってきます。
   this / every winter, / come / to / peaceful / monarch butterflies / millions of / forest

6. この世界遺産の場所はメキシコのどこに位置しますか。
   where / located / in / this / World Heritage Site / is / Mexico / ?

COFFEE BREAK

What do Butterflies Represent?
「蝶は何を象徴しているか」

その豪華な色合いのため、蝶は美の象徴となっています。蝶はとても優雅に舞うので、その舞いはダンスを表します。もし、蝶があなたにとまれば、それは幸運を意味します。でも、もしあなたが緊張感を感じれば、英語では、胃の中に蝶がいる（butterflies in your stomach）と表します。

Chapter 5 ◆ The Migration of the Monarch Butterflies

VI Finding Errors

次の各文には語法または語彙上の誤りが2個所ずつあります。その個所に下線を引き、それを適切な語句に直し（　）内に記入しなさい。また、全文の日本語訳を書きなさい。

1. Guiding by the sun, Canada geese fly during the day, and resting at night.
　　　　　　　　　　　　　　　　（　　　　　　　）（　　　　　　　）

2. This migrate is true a miracle of nature.
　　　　　　　　　　　　　　　　（　　　　　　　）（　　　　　　　）

3. Some day my brother told me where the monarch butterflies had went.
　　　　　　　　　　　　　　　　（　　　　　　　）（　　　　　　　）

4. Between November to March, Mr. and Mrs. Smith are in California or Mexico where the whether is warm.
　　　　　　　　　　　　　　　　（　　　　　　　）（　　　　　　　）

5. Sudden the house was filling with millions of ants.
　　　　　　　　　　　　　　　　（　　　　　　　）（　　　　　　　）

VII Full Writing

次の日本語を英語に直しなさい。

1. 私は小さな少年の頃、虫を追いかけるのが大好きでした。

2. ある日、私は先生にその少年はどこに行ってしまったのか尋ねました。

3. 私たちが浜松市に到着するのにほぼ10時間かかります。

4. これらの特別なハンバーガーをどこで食べることができるでしょうか。

〈Cacao Pods〉

New Foods from the New World

〈新世界より〉

People are often surprised that many popular foods come from the Americas. To understand how they spread around the world and **what** they are, we have to briefly step back in history.

In 15th century Europe, the price of spices imported from India and the Far East had skyrocketed. Because of wars and economic rivalry, the land routes had become extremely dangerous. Since fewer shipments of spices arrived, the prices increased dramatically.

A few daring European explorers had an unconventional solution. To find the spices, they decided to travel to India and the Far East by sea rather than by land. The Portuguese sailed around Africa, and finally reached India. The Spanish instead went west across the Atlantic Ocean. **What** they found was not India, but rather a "New World," which they later named America.

Although the explorers did not find spices in America, they discovered new foods. **What** are they? They tasted corn grown in Mexico and potatoes cultivated in the mountains of Peru. They ate a native fruit called the tomato. They enjoyed sweet, juicy pineapples and creamy avocados. They liked the hot chili peppers.

Chocolate is **what** could be considered the most exotic food from the New World. The local population used the beans from the cacao tree to make a bitter drink called "chocolate." The Europeans added sugar, honey or spices to make it taste less bitter. In the 19th century, new techniques improved the texture and flavor of chocolate. Since then, people all around the world have been enjoying chocolate candy, chocolate cakes, chocolate ice cream and chocolate drinks.

Thanks to the explorers who carried back seeds and plants from the New World, Europeans discovered new foods. Since then, many of these American imports have become international favorites.

What are your favorite foods from the New World?

Chapter 6 ◆ New Foods from the New World

"MUST-KNOW" collocations and phrases

1. be surprised that ～　～で驚く
2. spread around the world　世界中に広まる
3. extremely dangerous　極めて危険な
4. by sea　海路で、船で
5. by land　陸路で
6. carry back　持ち帰る

I Comprehension Questions

本文の内容に合っている文にはTを、合っていない文にはFを(　)内に記入しなさい。

1. (　) The price of spices increased because fewer shipments arrived.
2. (　) The European explorers liked the new spices they found in the "New World."
3. (　) At first, chocolate was a bitter drink.

II Guided Summary

次の英文は本文を要約したものです。(1)から(10)の空所に、下の(a)-(j)から適語を選んで記入し文を完成させなさい。

Many (1) _____ foods come from the New World. In the 15th century, the price of spices, imported from India and the East, had (2) _____. A few daring European (3) _____ thought they could go to India and the Far East by sea rather than by land. The Portuguese (4) _____ around Africa and arrived in India. The Spanish went west across the Atlantic Ocean, and found (5) _____. It was not India but a "New World" which they later named America. There were no spices. Instead they (6) _____ new foods such as corn, potatoes, tomatoes, pineapples, avocados and (7) _____ peppers. The most (8) _____ food was chocolate. At first, chocolate was a bitter drink. Now it is used to make (9) _____, ice cream and candies. Thanks to these explorers, many of these American "imports" have become international (10) _____.

[(a) sailed   (b) cakes   (c) chili   (d) popular   (e) favorites
  (f) land   (g) exotic   (h) skyrocketed (i) discovered (j) explorers]

 《whatの使い方》

◆「何」であるかを尋ねる what（疑問詞の what）

何であるかを尋ねる場合は、疑問詞の what を使います。直接疑問文では、what の後ろは疑問文の語順となり、間接疑問文では、平叙文の語順となります。

[直接疑問文]

ex 1) **What** are they?（本文第4段落）

ex 2) **What** are your favorite foods?（本文第7段落）

直接疑問文は、「what＋動詞＋主語」の語順となります。これら2つの例は、いずれも be 動詞が使われる例文です。一方、一般動詞を使った文は、次のように「what＋助動詞＋主語＋動詞」の語順になります。

What do you like?（あなたは何が好きですか）

[間接疑問文]

ex 3) To understand how they spread around the world and **what** they are, we have to briefly step back in history.（本文第1段落）

what they are の部分が、間接疑問文となっていて、語順は「what＋主語＋動詞」となります。

◆「～すること（もの）」を表す what（関係代名詞の what）

関係代名詞の what は先行詞をその中に含みます。what は the thing(s) which と言い換えることができます。

What he said confused us.（彼が言ったことは、私たちを混乱させた）

What を The thing which と置き換えて、The thing which he said confused us. とすることもできます。

ex 4) **What** they found was not India.（本文第3段落）

what they found で「彼らが見つけたもの」の意味。the thing they found と置き換えることができます。

◆ その他の what を用いた表現

目的などを尋ねる時に、What ... for?（何のために？）を使うことがあります。

What did you say that **for**?（何のためにあなたはあんなことを言ったの？）

Why did you say that? と同様の意味を表します。誰かの発言に対する返答として、「何のために？」という意味で次のように What for? だけで使うこともしばしばあります。

A: I went to Tokyo last Saturday.（私は先週の土曜日、東京に行ってきました）

B: **What for?**（何のために？）

III Warming up for Writing

（1）次の一連の文字群を、適切に切り離し英文を完成しなさい。ただし〈　〉内の単語が欠落しているので適所に補いなさい。

1. Peopleoftensurprisedthatmanypopularfoodscometheamericas. 〈are, from〉
   _____

2. ChocolateiscouldbeconsideredmostexoticfoodfromtheNewWorld. 〈what, the〉
   _____

（2）次の日本語に相当する英語表現になるように（　）に適語を書きなさい。

1. 驚く
   be (　　　　)
2. 歴史をさかのぼる
   (　　　　)(　　　　) in history
3. インドから輸入されたスパイス
   spices (　　　　)(　　　　) India
4. 極東
   (　　　　) East
5. 大西洋を越えて
   (　　　　) the (　　　　) Ocean
6. インドではなく「新世界」
   (　　　　) India, (　　　　) rather a "New World"
7. メキシコで育てられたトウモロコシ
   corn (　　　　) in Mexico
8. ～のおかげで
   (　　　　) to ～

IV Slash Writing

日本語を見ながら音声を聴き、英文を書き取りなさい。　CD 29~31

1. 理解するために / それらがどのように世界中に広まったか / そしてそれらが何であるかを / 私たちは少しさかのぼる必要がある / 歴史の中を
   To _____ / how they _____ around the world /
   and _____ they are, / we have to briefly step back / in _____.

2. 戦争や経済的競争のため / 陸路はなっていました / 極めて危険に
   Because of _____ and economic _____, /
   the land _____ had _____ / extremely dangerous.

3. 彼らが発見したものは / インドではなかった / しかしそれどころか / 「新世界」だった / 後に彼らはアメリカと名付けた
   _____ they found / was not _____, / but _____ /
   a "New World," / which they later _____ America.

V Word Order

日本語を参考にして下にある語句を並べ替え英文を完成しなさい。

1. あのレストランでのあなたの好きな食べ物は何ですか。
   are / restaurant / what / favorite / your / that / foods / in / ?

   _____

2. バスコ・ダ・ガマは、アフリカの周りを航海し、ついにインドに到達しました。
   around / reached / sailed / Vasco da Gama / India / Africa, / and / finally

   _____

3. 彼らが見つけたのはインドではなくアメリカでした。
   but / they / what / was / found / not / America / India

   _____

4. 彼らは、メキシコで育てられているトウモロコシや、ペルーの山々で栽培されているジャガイモを楽しみました。
   corn / grown in Mexico, / potatoes / cultivated / and / they enjoyed / in the mountains / of Peru

   _____

5. 彼らは、甘くてみずみずしいパイナップルややわらかなアボカドを味わいました。
   tasted / and / pineapples / avocados / they / juicy / sweet, / creamy

   _____

6. 新世界からのもっとも異国情緒あふれる食べ物であると考えられたであろうものは、チョコレートでした。
   could / what / food / be considered / exotic / the most / from the New World / is chocolate

   _____

Wonderful Tomato
「素晴らしきトマト」

トマトは、ヨーロッパの探検家たちが「新世界」から持ち帰った最も人気のある食料品です。今日では、世界中の人がトマトを食べています。トマトは、育てやすく、調理しても生でも美味しいし、健康にもよいと、いいこと尽くめです。

Chapter 6 ◆ New Foods from the New World

VI Finding Errors

次の各文には語法または語彙上の誤りが2個所ずつあります。その個所に下線を引き、それを適切な語句に直し（　）内に記入しなさい。また、全文の日本語訳を書きなさい。

1. In order to know how they spread around the world and what there are, we have to brief step back in history.
　　　　　　　　　　　　　　　　　(　　　　　　　) (　　　　　　　)

2. As of wars and economic rivalry, the land routes had became quite dangerous.
　　　　　　　　　　　　　　　　　(　　　　　　　) (　　　　　　　)

3. The land the Spanish explorers founded was not India, but rather a land which would be late called America.
　　　　　　　　　　　　　　　　　(　　　　　　　) (　　　　　　　)

4. For the local populations, chocolate was a drink make from cacao beans.
　　　　　　　　　　　　　　　　　(　　　　　　　) (　　　　　　　)

5. After then, chocolate has been used to cakes, ice cream and candy.
　　　　　　　　　　　　　　　　　(　　　　　　　) (　　　　　　　)

VII Full Writing

次の日本語を英語に直しなさい。

1. 多くの学生がアメリカ大陸から来ていることに、人々はしばしば驚きます。

2. メキシコ人はトウモロコシを育て、ペルー人は山々でジャガイモを栽培しました。

3. アメリカに到達したヨーロッパ人たちはトマトと呼ばれるものを食べました。

4. アイルランドの主食は何ですか。

41

Foreign Language Study Makes You a Global Citizen

〈外国語学習は地球市民へのパスポート〉

CD 32

Students often complain that learning a foreign language is difficult. They are right. Sometimes they comment that life **would** be easier if everybody spoke the same language. As appealing as this hypothesis **may** sound, it is not realistic.

Languages always change. First, they change throughout the years. For example, the English we speak today is different from the English of 500 years ago. Second, languages change as people travel or migrate to new places. The varieties of English in the US and Australia are not the same as the English in the UK.

Sometimes a language changes so much that it becomes a "new" language. Latin, which was once the official language of the Roman Empire, eventually developed into several new languages: Italian, Spanish, Portuguese, French and Rumanian. We **must** accept the fact that languages, like people, change until they die.

Today there are more than 5,000 languages in the world. Of course, it's impossible to learn all of them. Nonetheless, you **should** try to master one or two so that you **can** communicate with people from different cultures. Then you discover that their worldview **may** not be the same as yours.

It is important to remember that the language you speak conditions how you think and how you behave. When you speak a second or third language, you realize that your values are not universal. This experience makes you more tolerant about differences, more open to new ideas and more excited to make new friends.

The rewards of foreign language study far outweigh the frustrations. People who are bi- or multilingual have a definite advantage over their monolingual counterparts. They are better equipped to deal with the challenges of the 21st century.

If you want to become a global citizen, you **should** study a foreign language.

"MUST-KNOW" collocations and phrases

1. the official language of the Roman Empire　ローマ帝国の公用語
2. of course　もちろん
3. tolerant about differences　違いについて寛容である
4. open to new ideas　新しい考えに対して開けている
5. make new friends　新しい友人を作る
6. the challenges of the 21st century　21世紀の課題

I Comprehension Questions

本文の内容に合っている文にはTを、合っていない文にはFを（　）内に記入しなさい。

1. (　) The English spoken today is not the same as the English spoken centuries ago.
2. (　) When languages stop changing, they die.
3. (　) Monolingual speakers are better equipped to be global citizens in the 21st century.

II Guided Summary

次の英文は本文を要約したものです。(1)から(10)の空所に、下の(a)-(j)から適語を選んで記入し文を完成させなさい。　♪CD 33

Foreign language study is difficult. Sometimes students (1) ＿＿＿＿＿ that life would be easier if everybody spoke the same language. This (2) ＿＿＿＿＿ is unrealistic because languages always change. They change (3) ＿＿＿＿＿ the years. They also change when people travel or (4) ＿＿＿＿＿ to new places. Sometimes, as in the case of Latin, a language changes into "new" languages. Today there are more than 5,000 languages spoken in the world. You can't learn all of them, but you should (5) ＿＿＿＿＿ one or two so that you can (6) ＿＿＿＿＿ with people from different (7) ＿＿＿＿＿. Bi- and (8) ＿＿＿＿＿ people are better equipped to deal with the (9) ＿＿＿＿＿ of the 21st century. If you want to be a (10) ＿＿＿＿＿ citizen, you should study a foreign language.

(a) migrate	(b) cultures	(c) comment	(d) global
(e) challenges	(f) multilingual	(g) throughout	(h) master
(i) hypothesis	(j) communicate		

Focus Point 《助動詞の使い方》

助動詞は、動詞の原形の前に置き、その動詞にいろいろな意味をつけ加える働きをします。

◆ would

will の過去形。また、if 節とともに用いられて「もし～ならば、…であろう」というニュアンスを表すこともあります。

ex 1) Sometimes they comment that life **would** be easier if everybody spoke the same language.（本文第1段落）
「もし皆が同じ言語を話したならば」という if 節とともに用いられ、would は「人生は楽になるだろう」の「～だろう」というニュアンスを表しています。

◆ may

「～してもよい」（許可）、「～かもしれない」（推量）などが may の代表的な意味。

ex 2) As appealing as this hypothesis **may** sound, it is not realistic.（本文第1段落）

ex 3) You discover that their worldview **may** not be the same as yours.（本文第4段落）
ここの助動詞 may は「～かもしれない」というニュアンスを表します。

◆ must

must は、する必要があることを表す時に使い、「～しなければならない」という意味を表します。

ex 4) We **must** accept the fact that languages, like people, change until they die.（本文第3段落）
must accept the fact で「事実を受け入れなければならない」の意味。

◆ can

can は「～できる」（可能）、「ありうる」（可能性）などの意味を表します。

ex 5) You **should** try to master one or two so that you **can** communicate with people from different cultures.（本文第4段落）
この文の can は「～できる」という可能の意味で使われています。

◆ should

should は、何をしたらよいか助言する時に使い、「～すべきである」という意味を表します。
ex 5) の例文では、「1つか2つの言語をマスターしようと努力すべきである」という意味で使われています。

ex 6) If you want to become a global citizen, you **should** study a foreign language.（本文第7段落）
「外国語を勉強すべきである」の「～すべき」という意味で使われています。

III Warming up for Writing

(1) 次の一連の文字群を、適切に切り離し英文を完成しなさい。ただし〈　〉内の単語が欠落しているので適所に補いなさい。

1. Studentsoftencomplainlearningaforeignlanguagedifficult.〈that, is〉
   _____

2. Asappealingthishypothesissounditisnotrealistic.〈as, may〉
   _____

(2) 次の日本語に相当する英語表現になるように（　）に適語を書きなさい。

1. 外国語を学ぶこと
   (　　　　) a foreign language
2. 人生はより楽であろう
   life would be (　　　　)
3. 500年前の英語
   the English (　　　　) 500 years
   (　　　　)
4. それらが死ぬまで
   (　　　　) they die
5. 異文化出身の人たち
   people (　　　　) different (　　　　)
6. あなたが話す言語
   the language you (　　　　)
7. 〜をはるかに勝る
   far (　　　　) 〜
8. 地球市民
   a (　　　　) (　　　　)

IV Slash Writing

日本語を見ながら音声を聴き、英文を書き取りなさい。　🎧 34~36

1. 時には彼らは言います / 人生はより楽になる / もし皆が同じ言語を話したならば
   Sometimes they _____ that / life _____ be _____ /
   if everybody _____ the same language.

2. 例えば / 今日私たちが話す英語は / 英語と違います / 500年前の
   For _____, / the English we _____ today /
   is _____ _____ the English / of _____ years ago.

3. 私たちは事実を受け入れなければなりません / 言語は、人間同様 / 死ぬまで変わる
   We _____ accept the fact / that languages, _____ _____, /
   change until they _____.

V Word Order

日本語を参考にして下にある語句を並べ替え英文を完成しなさい。

1. この提案は魅力的に聞こえるかもしれませんが、それは現実的ではありません。
   appealing / may sound, / it / not realistic / this proposal / is / as / as

2. 言語は、人々が新しい場所に移動したり移住したりするに連れて、変わります。
   languages / migrate / people / as / to new places / or / change / travel

3. 今日、世界には190以上の国家があります。
   nations / are / in / more than 190 / the / there / today / world

4. あなたは彼らの価値観があなたのものとは同じでないかもしれないとわかります。
   not / may / be / you / discover that / yours / the same as / their values

5. 外国語学習の報いは、そのフラストレーションよりもはるかに勝ります。
   of / frustrations / foreign language / study / far / the rewards / the / outweigh

6. もし地球市民になりたければ、あなたは外国語を勉強すべきです。
   you / a global citizen, / you / if / should / a foreign language / study / want to become

A New Kind of English
「新種の英語」

科学技術が英語を変化させています。私たちが、メールを打ったり、チャットしたり、インスタントメッセージをしたりする場合は、時間とスペースを節約する必要があります。だから、私たちは、略語やシンボルや顔文字や絵文字などの近道を使います。今日では、このような新種の英語を定義しているオンライン辞書もあります。それは、あなたがコンヤ（2nite＝tonight, 今夜）やアシタ（2moro＝tomorrow, 明日）チェックできるから、スバラシイ（GR8＝GREAT, 素晴らしい）。それらは、イツデモ（24/7＝24 hours a day for the 7 days of the week, 週7日間毎日24時間）使えます。デハ、サヨウナラ（B4N＝Bye for now, では、さようなら）。

VI Finding Errors

次の各文には語法または語彙上の誤りが2個所ずつあります。その個所に下線を引き、それを適切な語句に直し（　）内に記入しなさい。また、全文の日本語訳を書きなさい。

1. Japanese students often complaint that learn a foreign language is difficult.
(　　　　　　) (　　　　　　)

2. Sometimes students comment that life to be easier if everybody spoken the same language.
(　　　　　　) (　　　　　　)

3. Sometimes a language changes so little that it becoming a "new" language.
(　　　　　　) (　　　　　　)

4. We have to accept the fact that languages, likes people, change until they'll die.
(　　　　　　) (　　　　　　)

5. People whose are bi- or multilingual have an advantage of their monolingual counterparts.
(　　　　　　) (　　　　　　)

VII Full Writing

次の日本語を英語に直しなさい。

1. 学生たちは、第2言語または第3言語を学ぶことは難しいとしばしば不平を言います。

2. 私たちは、異文化出身の人々とのコミュニケーションは難しいという事実を受け入れなければなりません。

3. もしあなたが試験に合格したければ、あなたはとても一生懸命に勉強するべきである。

4. 異文化出身の新しい友達を作ることが、外国語学習の報いの一つです。

Isaac Lufkin:
The Armless Football Player

〈両腕のないフットボーラー〉

The fans went wild every time the Purples, the freshman football team from Classical High School, made a goal. They called out words of encouragement to all the players, but especially to Isaac, their talented kicker. When the exciting game ended, the Purples had crushed their opponents with a score of 41 to 20!

Winning the final game was important for the team. This victory meant that their dream of **playing** an undefeated season and **earning** the freshman state title had come true. The Purples were indeed the champions for 2013.

Winning the final game was also important for Isaac Lufkin, the team's kicker. This teen had been born without arms. Despite his disability, he was a respected member of the Purples. **Playing** football made him feel like the other boys. Frankly **speaking**, nobody likes **being** different.

Isaac was lucky to have a strong, caring mother. She wanted her son to be able to take care of himself and not to depend on others. Whenever he said, "I can't do it," she always replied, "Yes, you can do it!"

Isaac listened to his mother's advice. By the time he was six, he was **washing**, **dressing**, and **feeding** himself. He learned to use his toes for **texting**, **playing** video games, and **working** on the computer. Thanks to his strong legs, he is now a star kicker. One day he hopes to play for the NFL!

The inspiring story of Isaac Lufkin, the armless football player, has gone viral. His positive "can-do" attitude has inspired people everywhere. A few months after the Purples' victory, President Barack Obama sent Isaac a letter **congratulating** him on his courage and determination to overcome his disability.

Isaac Lufkin is a very special young man. By **following** his "can-do" attitude, we too can make our dreams come true.

Chapter 8 ◆ Isaac Lufkin: The Armless Football Player

"MUST-KNOW" collocations and phrases

1. word(s) of encouragement 激励の言葉
2. despite one's disability 体が不自由であるにもかかわらず
3. frankly speaking 率直に言えば
4. go viral 拡散する、口コミで広まる
5. a can-do attitude やる気満々の姿勢
6. determination to overcome one's disability 障害を乗り越える決意

I Comprehension Questions

本文の内容に合っている文にはTを、合っていない文にはFを( )内に記入しなさい。

1. (   ) The Purples played an undefeated season and earned the freshman state title.
2. (   ) Isaac's mother taught her son how to take care of himself.
3. (   ) Few people know about Isaac's inspiring story.

II Guided Summary

次の英文は本文を要約したものです。(1)から(10)の空所に、下の(a)-(j)から適語を選んで記入し文を完成させなさい。 CD 38

The fans went (1) _____ when the Purples, the freshman football team from Classical High School, won the final game. This victory meant that their dream of (2) _____ an undefeated season and (3) _____ the freshman state title had come true. This (4) _____ was also very important for Isaac Lufkin, the team's (5) _____ kicker who had been born without arms. Isaac's mother taught him how to take (6) _____ of himself. When he could not do something, she told him, "Yes, you can do it." The (7) _____ story of Isaac, the armless football player, has gone (8) _____. The US President Barack Obama wrote Isaac a letter of (9) _____. We should follow Isaac's (10) _____.

    (a) care   (b) earning   (c) example   (d) inspiring   (e) congratulations
    (f) wild   (g) viral   (h) victory   (i) playing   (j) talented

49

Focus Point 《動名詞と現在分詞の使い方》

◆ 動名詞
動名詞を作るには動詞を～ing 形にします。動名詞の働きは次の４つです。
- ① 主　　　　　語：**Texting** is fun.（携帯メールをすることは楽しい）
- ② be 動詞の補語：My hobby is **playing** the guitar.（私の趣味はギターを弾くことです）
- ③ 他動詞の目的語：We enjoyed **playing** tennis.（私たちはテニスをすることを楽しみました）
- ④ 前置詞の目的語：She is afraid of **making** mistakes.
　　　　　　　　　　（彼女は間違いをすることをおそれています）

ex 1) Their dream of **playing** an undefeated season and (of) **earning** the freshman state title had come true.（本文第２段落）
　　 playing, earning ともに前置詞 of の後に置かれ、「～の試合をする夢」、「～を獲得する夢」と of の目的語となっています。（⇒ ④前置詞の目的語）

ex 2) **Winning** this final game was important for Isaac Lufkin.（本文第３段落）
　　 Winning this final game「この最終戦に勝つことは」と主語となっています。（⇒ ①主語）

ex 3) Nobody likes **being** different.（本文第３段落）
　　 この文における being は「特異であることを」を「誰も好まない」と他動詞 like の目的語となっています。（⇒ ③他動詞の目的語）

◆ 現在分詞
現在分詞の形は、動詞の原型に～ing をつけて、進行形（be＋～ing）の文で使われたり、「～している」や「～しながら」という意味を表し、形容詞的・副詞的な働きをしたりします。現在分詞の働きは次の４つです。

① **be 動詞と共に用い、現在進行形や過去進行形をつくる。**
ex 4) By the time he was six, he **was washing**, **dressing**, and **feeding** himself.（本文第５段落）

② **第５文型（SVOC）の補語（C）の働きをする。**
　　 I saw the girl **playing** the piano on the stage.
　　（私はその少女が舞台でピアノを弾いているのを見ました）

③ **「～している」「～する」という意味の「形容詞」として働き、前か後ろに置かれた名詞を修飾する。**
ex 5) President Barack Obama sent Isaac a letter **congratulating** him on his courage and determination to overcome his disability（本文第６段落）

④ **「～して」「～しながら」という意味の「副詞」として働き、前か後ろに置かれた文や動詞を修飾する。**
　　 The lady was looking at me **smiling**.（その夫人は微笑みながら私を見ていました）
　　　　　　　（見ていた）←（微笑みながら）
　　　　　　　＝前に置かれた動詞［was looking］を修飾しています。

Chapter 8　Isaac Lufkin: The Armless Football Player

III Warming up for Writing

（1）次の一連の文字群を、適切に切り離し英文を完成しなさい。ただし〈　〉内の単語が欠落しているので適所に補いなさい。

1. Thisvictorymeantthattheirdreamplayinganundefeatedseasonandearningthe freshmanstatetitlecometrue.〈of, had〉

   _____

2. Shewantedhersontobeabletakecareofhimselfandnottodependothers.〈to, on〉

   _____

（2）次の日本語に相当する英語表現になるように（　）に適語を書きなさい。

1. 熱狂する
   go (　　　)
2. 最終戦に勝つこと
   (　　　) the final (　　　)
3. 他人に頼る
   (　　　) on (　　　)
4. 彼の強靭な脚のおかげで
   (　　　)(　　　) his strong legs
5. （話などが）拡散する
   go (　　　)
6. やる気満々の姿勢
   a can-do (　　　)
7. いたるところで人々を奮い立たせる
   (　　　) people (　　　)
8. 夢を実現する
   (　　　) one's dream (　　　) true

IV Slash Writing

日本語を見ながら音声を聴き、英文を書き取りなさい。　　　39~41

1. 彼らは大声で叫んだ / 励ましの言葉を / すべての選手に、しかも特にアイザックに
   They _____ _____ / _____ of encouragement /
   to _____ the players, but _____ to Isaac.

2. 彼が6歳になる時までに / 彼は身体を洗って / 着替えをして / 自分で食事もしていた
   By the _____ he was _____, / he was _____, /
   _____, / and _____ himself.

3. アイザック・ラフキンの物語は / 口コミで広まりました。/ 彼の積極的なやる気満々の姿勢は / あらゆるところで人々を鼓舞しています
   The _____ _____ Isaac Lufkin /
   has gone _____. / His _____ "can-do" attitude /
   has _____ people everywhere.

V Word Order

日本語を参考にして下にある語句を並べ替え英文を完成しなさい。

1. 香川がゴールするたびにファンは熱狂しました。

   Kagawa / the fans / a goal / every time / made / wild / went

   _____

2. ワールド・シリーズでは常に、初戦に勝つことが大切です。

   game / winning / the first / is / in /always / important / the World Series

   _____

3. ビデオゲームで遊ぶことで彼は他の男の子たちと同じような気持ちになれました。

   video games / boys / playing / him / made / the other / like / feel

   _____

4. 彼女はいつも父親のアドバイスに耳を傾けました。

   she / father's / listened / her / always / to / advice

   _____

5. 彼の積極的な心構えは多くの人々に勇気を与えました。

   inspired / many / attitude / his / positive / people

   _____

6. オバマ大統領は彼の勇気を祝福する手紙をアイザックに出しました。

   President Obama / Isaac / him / sent / congratulating / a letter / his courage / on

   _____

COFFEE BREAK

The same story but 50 years earlier
「全く同じ話が50年前に」

両腕がない状態で生まれたアイザックと同じ障害を持った少年クリスが、アイザックと同じクラシカル・ハイ・スクールで、しかも同じくアメリカンフットボールの名キッカーとして活躍し、彼もまた当時の大統領より祝福の手紙を1963年（50年前）にもらっているとは何と不思議な偶然なのでしょう。まさに「歴史は繰り返す」ですね。

VI Finding Errors

次の各文には語法上の誤りが2個所ずつあります。その個所に下線を引き、それを適切な語句に直し（　）内に記入しなさい。また、全文の日本語訳を書きなさい。

1. The fans went wild every times Honda make a goal.
   (　　　　　　　) (　　　　　　　)
   _____

2. They called out words of encourage to all the players, but especial to Sawa.
   (　　　　　　　) (　　　　　　　)
   _____

3. Win this game was also importance for Nadeshiko Japan.
   (　　　　　　　) (　　　　　　　)
   _____

4. Frankly speak, no one likes be different.
   (　　　　　　　) (　　　　　　　)
   _____

5. By follow Isaac's "can-do" attitude, we can make our dreams came true.
   (　　　　　　　) (　　　　　　　)
   _____

VII Full Writing

次の日本語を英語に直しなさい。

1. 彼らは大声で叫んで、有能なキッカー、五郎丸に激励の言葉を贈りました。
   _____

2. 最終戦で勝つことは我がチームにとって重要なことでした。
   _____

3. 障害にもかかわらず、彼は自分の夢を実現することができました。
   _____

4. 率直に言えば、私は孤独なことを望みません。
   _____

Atlantis, the Lost Empire: Fact or Fiction?

〈失われたアトランティス帝国〉

Many centuries ago, the Greek philosopher Plato wrote a story about a mysterious island empire called Atlantis. According to Plato, it was once an earthly paradise. The rulers were wise and just. They traded with their neighbors, and never waged war. The people were kind, generous and loving. The capital of this empire was a magnificent city with marvelous buildings and fantastic treasures.

Unfortunately as the years passed, the Atlanteans forgot the peaceful ways of the past. They became greedy, corrupt and cruel. They fought wars against their neighbors. Then one day, there was a tremendous volcanic eruption followed by a killer tsunami. In less than 24 hours, Atlantis disappeared forever.

Since that tragic moment, adventurers and scholars **have been trying** to locate Atlantis. They **have been searching** all over the world for this lost empire, but to no avail. Nobody **has been able to** answer the question. Is the story of Atlantis fact or fiction?

The Greek island of Santorini may give us some clues for solving this mystery. Scholars, archaeologists and geologists know that around 1500 BC, the volcano on Santorini erupted violently. Part of the island sank into the sea.

Recent excavations on Santorini **have uncovered** a huge, well-planned city under the volcanic ash. Many homes are decorated with gorgeous frescoes, and have modern conveniences such as hot and cold running water and even indoor bathrooms. For some people, this buried city is, in fact, the lost empire of Atlantis.

For others, the story of Atlantis is only fiction, not fact. In either case, it teaches us an important lesson about human behavior. If greed, corruption and cruelty control our hearts, then one day they will erupt and destroy us.

So maybe the story of Atlantis is both fact and fiction.

Chapter 9 ◆ Atlantis, the Lost Empire: Fact or Fiction?

"MUST-KNOW" collocations and phrases

1. the Greek philosopher Plato ギリシャの哲学者プラトン（BC427-BC347）
2. an earthly paradise 地上の楽園
3. wage war 戦争をしかける
4. tremendous volcanic eruption 巨大な火山の爆発
5. a killer tsunami 犠牲者を出す津波
6. volcanic ash 火山灰

I Comprehension Questions

本文の内容に合っている文にはTを、合っていない文にはFを（　）内に記入しなさい。

1. (　) Atlantis was destroyed by a tremendous volcanic eruption followed by a killer tsunami.
2. (　) Everybody believes that the city buried under the volcanic ash on Santorini is Atlantis.
3. (　) The story of Atlantis teaches that greed, corruption and cruelty can destroy human beings.

II Guided Summary

次の英文は本文を要約したものです。(1)から(10)の空所に、下の(a)-(j)から適語を選んで記入し文を完成させなさい。

Many (1) _____ ago, the Greek philosopher Plato wrote a story about Atlantis. This (2) _____ island empire was once an "earthly (3) _____" with marvelous buildings and fantastic treasures. The rulers were (4) _____, and the people were kind. Unfortunately as the years passed, they became greedy, (5) _____ and cruel. One day after a tremendous volcanic (6) _____ and a killer tsunami, Atlantis disappeared. Since then, nobody has been able to find Atlantis. The Greek island of Santorini may give us some (7) _____. Thousands of years ago, the volcano on this island erupted. Recently archaeologists have (8) _____ a huge city under the volcanic ash. Some believe that this is the lost empire of Atlantis. Others are not (9) _____. But everyone agrees that the story of Atlantis teaches an important lesson about human (10) _____.

[
(a) wise　　　(b) clues　　　(c) convinced　　(d) eruption　　(e) mysterious
(f) uncovered　(g) corrupt　　(h) centuries　　(i) behavior　　(j) paradise
]

55

Focus Point 《現在完了形と現在完了進行形の使い方》

◆ 現在完了形

現在完了は、have[has]＋過去分詞の形で、「完了」「結果」「経験」「継続」などの意味を表します。過去の出来事が何らかの形で現在に影響を与えているというニュアンスを表しています。

① **完了**「もう～してしまった」「今～したところだ」など、現在までに動作が完了したことを表す。
I **have finished** my homework.（私は宿題を終えてしまった）

② **結果**「～している」「～して今は…だ」など、過去の動作の後の、現在における結果を表す。
Summer **has come**.（夏がやってきました）

③ **経験**「これまでに～したことがある」など現在までの経験を表す。
I **have been** to New York.（私はニューヨークに行ったことがあります）

④ **継続**「～している」など過去から現在までの継続を表す。
I **have lived** in Okayama for 20 years now.（私は岡山に住んで今や20年になります）

ex 1) Recent excavations on Santorini **have uncovered** a huge, well-planned city under the volcanic ash.（本文第5段落）
最近の発掘調査の結果、火山灰の下にしっかりと計画された街が「見つかった」という結果を伝える文です。（⇒ ②結果）

ex 2) Nobody **has been able to** answer the question.（本文第3段落）
nobody が主語となる否定文で、「誰も～した経験がない」ということを表します。（⇒ ③経験）

◆ 現在完了進行形

現在完了形にも「継続」の意味がありますが、その継続のニュアンスが強く「ずっと～している」ということを表すのに現在完了進行形が使われます。現在完了進行形は、助動詞 have の現在形（have または has）＋been＋動詞の現在分詞（～ing）の形をとります。

I **have been studying**.（私はずっと勉強しています）
They **have been dating**.（彼らはずっと付き合っています）

ex 3) Since that tragic moment, adventurers and scholars **have been trying** to locate Atlantis.（本文第3段落）

ex 4) They **have been searching** all over the world for this lost empire, but to no avail.（本文第3段落）
上記2つの文とも失われたアトランティス大陸を求めて関係者が「ずっと探し続けている」というニュアンスを伝えています。

Chapter 9 ◆ Atlantis, the Lost Empire: Fact or Fiction?

III Warming up for Writing

（1）次の一連の文字群を、適切に切り離し英文を完成しなさい。ただし〈　〉内の単語が欠落しているので適所に補いなさい。

1. AccordingPlatoitwasonceanparadise.〈to, earthly〉

_____

2. Thattragicmomentadventurersandscholarshavetryingtolocate Atlantis.
〈since, been〉

_____

（2）次の日本語に相当する英語表現になるように（　）に適語を書きなさい。

1. アトランティスと呼ばれる不思議な島の帝国
   a mysterious (　　　) (　　　) called Atlantis

2. プラトンによると
   (　　　) (　　　) Plato

3. 〜に対して戦争を戦う
   (　　　) wars (　　　) 〜

4. 24時間以内に
   in (　　　) (　　　) 24 hours

5. 永遠に姿を消す
   (　　　) forever

6. しかし無駄である
   but to (　　　) (　　　)

7. 海中に沈む
   (　　　) (　　　) the sea

8. いずれにせよ
   (　　　) (　　　) case

IV Slash Writing

日本語を見ながら音声を聴き、英文を書き取りなさい。　🎧 44~46

1. この帝国の首都は / 巨大都市でした / 素晴らしい建物がある / そして素敵な宝も
   The _____ of this empire / was a _____ city /
   with _____ buildings / and fantastic _____.

2. 彼らはずっと探しています / 世界中を / この失われた帝国を求めて / しかし無駄である
   They have _____ _____ / all over the _____ /
   for this _____ empire, / but _____ no avail.

3. 最近のサントリニでの発掘は / 発見しました / 巨大なきっちりと計画された都市を / 火山灰の下に
   Recent _____ on Santorini / have _____ /
   a _____, well-planned city / under the volcanic _____.

V Word Order

日本語を参考にして下にある語句を並べ替え英文を完成しなさい。

1. プラトンによると、それは、かつては地上の楽園でした。
   to / an / once / was / according / earthly paradise / it / Plato,

2. 私は既に夏休みの宿題を終えてしまった。
   have / homework / my / I / vacation / finished / already / summer

3. 誰もその質問に答えられていません。
   has / question / answer / nobody / to / the / able / been

4. ネッシーの話は事実でしょうか、それとも虚構でしょうか。
   or / the / fact / is / Nessie / story / of / fiction / ?

5. DNA 鑑定の結果がこの謎を解く手がかりを私たちに与えるかもしれません。
   give us / may / this mystery / for solving / the results / DNA testing / of / some clues

6. よく計画された福井県での発掘が、巨大な恐竜の化石を発見しました。
   excavations / huge dinosaurs / uncovered / have / well-planned / of / in Fukui Prefecture / fossils

You Can Visit Atlantis
「アトランティス訪問は可能です」

バハマの贅沢なリゾートであるアトランティスでは、「地上の楽園」の楽しみを享受することができます。もし、ここが遠すぎるようならば、代わりにドバイのパーム・アイランドにある豪華なアトランティス・リゾートに行くこともできます。宿泊料が高い水中スイート・ルームの予約を忘れないように。そこでは、再現されたアトランティスの街を魚が泳ぐ姿が見られます。

VI Finding Errors

次の各文には語法または語彙上の誤りが2個所ずつあります。その個所に下線を引き、それを適切な語句に直し（　）内に記入しなさい。また、全文の日本語訳を書きなさい。

1. Unfortunately as the years past, they forgot the peaceful ways of the passed.
   (　　　　　　　) (　　　　　　　)

2. Then some day, there was a tremendous volcanic eruption followed as a killer tsunami.
   (　　　　　　　) (　　　　　　　)

3. In least than 24 hours, the island empire disappeared whatever.
   (　　　　　　　) (　　　　　　　)

4. Adventurers and scholars have been searching all over the world out this lost ship, but to no available.
   (　　　　　　　) (　　　　　　　)

5. They has been dating from February of this year.
   (　　　　　　　) (　　　　　　　)

VII Full Writing

次の日本語を英語に直しなさい。

1. 浦島太郎によると、それは、水中の楽園であった。

2. 学者たちは邪馬台国の位置を突き止めようとずっと懸命に努力している。

3. そしてある日、巨大ハリケーンがあり、続いて洪水がありました。

4. もし、欲望、腐敗、そして残虐がその国を支配しているのであるならば、その国はいつの日か永遠に消え去るであろう。

Pope Francis: A New Kind of Pope

〈新たな法王誕生〉

While you are visiting Rome, you will certainly want to see St. Peter's Basilica, the Vatican Museum and the Sistine Chapel. To reach them, you must enter St. Peter's Square. **As soon as** you cross the white line on the edge of this square, you are leaving Rome and entering the Vatican City.

Although the Vatican City is located inside the city of Rome, it is an independent nation. It is the smallest country in the world both in size (0.44 square km) and in population (842). The leader of this tiny state is the Pope, who is also the spiritual leader of more than 1.2 billion Christians.

On March 13, 2013, a new Pope was elected. In every sense of the word, Pope Francis is new. He was born in Argentina, and thus is the first Pope to come from the Americas. He is also the first Pope called Francis.

The new Pope chose this name in honor of St. Francis of Assisi. This beloved saint lived in poverty **even though** his family was wealthy. He helped the poor and the sick, and reminded people to respect nature.

Pope Francis wants to follow the saint's example. Instead of the luxurious Papal apartments, the new Pope lives in the more modest guesthouse. He reaches out to the poor, prays with the sick, and meets with the homeless. He loves children **because** he sees in them hope for the future. Like St. Francis, he believes that we must protect the environment.

Pope Francis understands the importance of technology. He uses it **so that** he can reach out to people of different backgrounds and different faiths. In his opinion, communication is the key to building bridges of understanding.

Even if Francis is a new kind of Pope, he must balance innovation and change with respect for tradition.

Chapter 10 ◆ Pope Francis: A New Kind of Pope

"MUST-KNOW" collocations and phrases

1. an independent nation 独立国家
2. the smallest country in the world 世界最小国家
3. hope for the future 未来への希望
4. protect the environment 環境を保護する
5. the importance of technology テクノロジーの重要性
6. build bridges of understanding 理解の橋を架ける

I Comprehension Questions

本文の内容に合っている文にはTを、合っていない文にはFを(　)内に記入しなさい。

1. (　) St. Peter's Basilica and the Sistine Chapel are located in the city of Rome.
2. (　) Like St. Francis of Assisi, the new Pope wants to help the poor and protect the environment.
3. (　) Pope Francis must try to find a balance between innovation and tradition.

II Guided Summary

次の英文は本文を要約したものです。(1)から(10)の空所に、下の(a)-(j)から適語を選んで記入し文を完成させなさい。

St. Peter's Basilica, the Vatican Museum and the Sistine Chapel are in the Vatican City. This tiny (1) _____ country is located inside the city of Rome. The head of state is the Pope, who is also the (2) _____ leader of more than 1.2 billion Christians. On March 13, 2013, Pope Francis was (3) _____. He is the first Pope from the Americas. He is also the first Pope called Francis. The new Pope chose this name in (4) _____ of St. Francis of Assisi. Like this famous saint, the new Pope wants to help the poor, pray with the sick, and (5) _____ nature. Pope Francis also understands the importance of (6) _____. He uses it to reach out to people of different (7) _____ and different faiths. For him, communication builds (8) _____ of understanding. Pope Francis must balance (9) _____ with respect for (10) _____.

```
(a) technology    (b) honor      (c) bridges     (d) independent
(e) backgrounds   (f) tradition  (g) elected     (h) innovation
(i) protect       (j) spiritual
```

《接続詞の使い方》

◆ 時を示す接続詞

時を表す接続詞で、最も一般的なものは when (～する時に) です (p.20 の Focus Point 参照)。他方、ある「期間」を表すのが while であり、「～するやいなや」「～するとすぐに」のような意味を示す代表的な接続詞句が as soon as です。

ex 1) **While** you are visiting Rome, you will certainly want to see St. Peter's Basilica. (本文第 1 段落)
「あなたがローマを訪問している間に」「あなたのローマ訪問期間中に」などの意味を表します。

ex 2) **As soon as** you cross the white line on the edge of this square, you are leaving Rome and entering the Vatican City. (本文第 1 段落)
「あなたが白線を越えるとすぐに」「あなたが白線を越えるやいなや」などの意味を表します。

◆ 原因・理由を示す接続詞

原因・理由を示す接続詞で最も一般的なものが because です。

ex 3) He loves children **because** he sees in them hope for the future. (本文第 5 段落)
「なぜならば～だからである」と主節の動詞（ここでは love(s)）の理由を説明しています。

◆ 目的を示す接続詞

so that＋主語＋can[may, will] ～で「…（主語）が～するために」という意味を表します。

ex 4) He uses it [technology] **so that** he can reach out to people of different backgrounds and different faiths. (本文第 6 段落)
「彼が人々に手を差し伸べることができるために」という意味になります。

◆ 譲歩を示す接続詞

although と though が「～だけれども」などと譲歩を表す接続詞の代表格です。また、even though または even if で「たとえ～であっても」という譲歩の意味を表します。

ex 5) **Although** the Vatican City is located inside the city of Rome, it is an independent nation. (本文第 2 段落)
「バチカン市国はローマ市内に位置しますが」という譲歩を表します。

ex 6) This beloved saint lived in poverty **even though** his family was wealthy. (本文第 4 段落)

ex 7) **Even if** Francis is a new kind of Pope, he must balance innovation and change with respect for tradition. (本文第 7 段落)
ex 6) では「彼の家族がたとえ裕福であっても」、ex 7) では「たとえフランシスは新しいタイプの法王であったとしても」という意味になります。

III Warming up for Writing

（1）次の一連の文字群を、適切に切り離し英文を完成しなさい。ただし〈 〉内の単語が欠落しているので適所に補いなさい。

1. WhileyouareRomeyouwillcertainlywantseeStPeter'sBasilica. 〈visiting, to〉
   _____

2. Itissmallestcountryintheworldinsizeandinpopulation. 〈the, both〉
   _____

（2）次の日本語に相当する英語表現になるように（ ）に適語を書きなさい。

1. 白線を越える
   (　　　) the white line
2. バチカン市国に入る
   (　　　) the Vatican City
3. どんな意味からも
   in (　　　) (　　　) of the word
4. 〜に敬意を示して
   in (　　　) of 〜
5. 貧困の中で暮らす
   live (　　　) (　　　)
6. 自然を敬う
   (　　　) nature
7. 病人たちとともに祈る
   (　　　) with (　　　) sick
8. 異なった背景の人々
   people of (　　　) (　　　)

IV Slash Writing

日本語を見ながら音声を聴き、英文を書き取りなさい。　🆑 49~51

1. この小国家の元首は / 法王です / その人はさらに / 宗教的リーダー / 12億人以上のキリスト教徒の
   The leader of this _____ state / is the _____, / who is also / the _____ leader / of more than 1.2 _____ Christians.

2. バチカン市国は、だけれども / ローマ市内に位置している / それは独立国家である
   _____ the Vatican City / is _____ inside the _____ of Rome, / it is an _____ nation.

3. この愛されていた聖人は / 貧しさの中生活していた / たとえ彼の家族が / 裕福であっても
   This _____ saint / lived in _____ / _____ _____ his family / was _____ .

V Word Order

日本語を参考にして下にある語句を並べ替え英文を完成しなさい。

1. 私たちが、広場の端の白線を越えるとすぐに、ローマを離れ、バチカン市国に入ることになります。
   as soon as / are / on the edge of this square, / leaving Rome / we / the white line / and entering the Vatican City / we cross

2. 彼女はたくさん勉強をしていますが、成績はよくありません。
   gets / she / she / although / grades / studies / a lot, / poor

3. フランシス法王は、貧しき者たちに手を差し伸べ、病める者たちと祈り、住むところなき者たちと会います。
   Pope Francis / and meets / with / reaches out to / the poor, / prays with / the sick, / the homeless

4. 彼は、子どもたちを愛しています。なぜならば彼らの姿に未来の希望を見ているからです。
   because / he sees / loves children, / he / the future / for / in them / hope

5. 聖フランシスのように、彼は、私たちが環境を保護すべきであると信じています。
   believes / he / that / like St. Francis / protect / must / we / the environment

6. 私の考えでは、コミュニケーションが理解の橋を架けるための鍵です。
   of / in / understanding / my opinion, / communication / the key to / building bridges / is

COFFEE BREAK

The Smallest Countries in the World
「世界の小国」

ご存知のように、バチカン市国が世界最小の国です。2番目に小さいのは、フランスに国境を接する公国モナコ（2平方キロメートル）です。3番目と4番目に小さい国家は、太平洋に浮かぶ2つの島国で、ナウル（21平方キロメートル）とツバル（26平方キロメートル）です。5番目は、イタリア国内に位置する共和国サンマリノ（61平方キロメートル）です。

VI Finding Errors

次の各文には語法または語彙上の誤りが2個所ずつあります。その個所に下線を引き、それを適切な語句に直し（　）内に記入しなさい。また、全文の日本語訳を書きなさい。

1. Through the Vatican City is locating inside the city of Rome, Italy, it is an independent nation.
(　　　　　　　) (　　　　　　　)

2. In November 4, 2008, President Obama was election.
(　　　　　　　) (　　　　　　　)

3. Edogawa Ranpo choose his pen name in humor of Edgar Allan Poe.
(　　　　　　　) (　　　　　　　)

4. St. Francis of Assisi lived in poor although his family was wealth.
(　　　　　　　) (　　　　　　　)

5. To his opinion, sympathy is the key to build bridges of understanding.
(　　　　　　　) (　　　　　　　)

VII Full Writing

次の日本語を英語に直しなさい。

1. ニューヨークに行ったら、あなたは、確実にセントラルパーク、タイムズスクエア、そして自由の女神を訪問したいと思うでしょう。

2. フランシス法王は、世界で最も小さな国のリーダーであるけれども、彼は、12億人以上のキリスト教徒の宗教的リーダーでもある。

3. その日、すべての選手はジャッキー・ロビンソン（Jackie Robinson）に敬意を表してユニフォームに番号「42」を身につけた。

4. 国連本部は厳密に言えばニューヨーク内に位置するが、それはアメリカ合衆国には属しません。

The Power of Meditation

〈瞑想の力〉

A familiar proverb tells us that you can't teach an old dog new tricks. In other words, it's hard, if not impossible, to change the way people think and act, especially as they age. Today neuroscientists don't agree. They have proof that you can indeed teach an "old" brain new tricks.

Until the 1970's, experts believed that the brain did not change after early childhood. Since then, studies have proof that an "old" brain can adapt to new situations, new information and new stimuli. Thanks to this discovery, new treatments are being developed for patients with brain injuries, strokes, chronic pain and even learning difficulties.

The good news does not stop here. Recent experiments point to the positive power of meditation. People who meditate concentrate **better** than those who don't. Individuals who meditate tend to be **less stressed**, **less anxious** and **less angry** than those who don't. It seems that meditation improves quality of life.

In Asia, meditation has been practiced for centuries. Now it has gone mainstream in many western countries. People understand that often it is **better** and **safer** than medication.

Today many Americans use Mindfulness Meditation as a way to reduce stress. To meditate, they sit comfortably with a straight back, place their hands on their thighs, and lower their eyes. As they breathe, they try to focus on "now." Slowly they begin to relax as they forget the distractions of daily life.

Mindfulness Meditation seems easy, but it is **more difficult** than you think. But for those who master the technique, it is well worth the effort. It has helped change how they think and how they behave. In short, the quality of their life is **better**.

So it seems that the neuroscientists are right. Sometimes you can teach an "old" brain new tricks.

Chapter 11 ◆ The Power of Meditation

"MUST-KNOW" collocations and phrases

1. after early childhood　幼少期以降
2. adapt to new situations　新しい状況に適応する
3. quality of life　生活の質、生命の質
4. with a straight back　背筋を伸ばして
5. distractions of daily life　日々の生活の雑念
6. in short　端的に言うと

I Comprehension Questions

本文の内容に合っている文にはTを、合っていない文にはFを（　）内に記入しなさい。

1. (　) It's hard, if not impossible, to change people, especially as they grow older.
2. (　) People who meditate concentrate less than those who don't.
3. (　) It seems easy to master the technique of Mindfulness Meditation, but that isn't true.

II Guided Summary

次の英文は本文を要約したものです。(1)から(10)の空所に、下の(a)-(j)から適語を選んで記入し文を完成させなさい。　　CD 53

According to a familiar (1) _____, you can't teach an old dog new tricks. Neuroscientists, however, don't (2) _____. They have (3) _____ that you can indeed teach an "old" brain new tricks. Today studies show that an "old" brain can (4) _____ to new situations, new information and new stimuli. Thanks to this discovery, there are new (5) _____ for patients with brain injuries, strokes, chronic pain and learning (6) _____. Meditation is important because it helps improve (7) _____ of life. In Asia, meditation has been practiced for centuries. Now it has gone (8) _____ in the West. Many Americans use Mindfulness Meditation to (9) _____ stress. It has helped change how they think and how they (10) _____. Their "old" brains are learning new tricks.

[
(a) proof　　(b) difficulties　(c) proverb　(d) reduce　　(e) quality
(f) behave　(g) adapt　　　(h) agree　　(i) mainstream　(j) treatments
]

《比較級の使い方》

2つのものを比較し、等しくない場合は、「形容詞（または副詞）の比較級＋than～」または「more＋形容詞（または副詞）＋than～」の形で表します。比較級の作り方は、以下のように分類できます。

◆ 形容詞の語尾に -er をつける場合

一音節の形容詞の場合は、語尾に -er をつけると比較級になります。例えば short（短い）は shorter となります。ただし e で終わる語は -r だけをつけると比較級となります。
My son runs **faster** than any other boy in his class.（私の息子はクラスのどの男子よりも速く走ります）

ex 1) People understand that often it is **better** and **safer** than medication.（本文第４段落）
safe は e で終わる語なので -r だけをつけています。

また、一音節の形容詞が、子音字＋母音字＋子音字の時、最後の子音字を重ねます。big → bigger
そして、形容詞が二音節で、-y で終わる時、-y を i に代えて -er をつけます。happy → happier

◆ 形容詞の前に more をつける場合

形容詞が三音節以上の時、形はそのままで、more＋形容詞とします。intelligent → more intelligent

ex 2) Mindfulness Meditation seems easy, but it is **more difficult** than you think.（本文第６段落）
difficult は三音節のため比較級は more difficult となっています。

◆ 不規則変化の場合

よく使われる形容詞や副詞は、不規則変化をとるものもあります。

ex 3) People who meditate concentrate **better** than those who don't.（本文第３段落）
better は副詞 well または形容詞 good の不規則変化の比較級です。この文では、副詞 well の比較級です。一方、ex 1) の文の better は形容詞 good の比較級です。

◆ less をつける劣等比較の場合

あるものが別のものより程度が低いことを示す時には、劣等比較を使います。「less＋形容詞（副詞）の原級＋than」の形になります。

ex 4) Individuals who meditate tend to be **less stressed**, **less anxious** and **less angry** than those who don't.（本文第３段落）
それぞれ stressed, anxious, angry の劣等比較になっています。

Chapter 11 ◆ The Power of Meditation

III Warming up for Writing

（1）次の一連の文字群を、適切に切り離し英文を完成しなさい。ただし〈　〉内の単語が欠落しているので適所に補いなさい。

1. Afamiliarproverbtellsusthatyoucan'tteachandogtricks.〈old, new〉
   _____

2. Peopleunderstandthatoftenitisandsafermedication.〈better, than〉
   _____

（2）次の日本語に相当する英語表現になるように（　）に適語を書きなさい。

1. 換言すると、言い換えると
   in (　　　) (　　　)
2. 特に彼らが年を取るにつれて
   especially as (　　　) (　　　)
3. 新しい状況に適応する
   (　　　) to new (　　　)
4. この発見のおかげで
   (　　　) (　　　) this discovery
5. 脳に損傷を負った患者
   patients (　　　) (　　　) injuries
6. 学習困難
   (　　　) difficulties
7. 多くの西洋諸国で
   in many (　　　) countries
8. ストレスを軽減する方法
   a way to (　　　) (　　　)

IV Slash Writing

日本語を見ながら音声を聴き、英文を書き取りなさい。　🎧 54~56

1. 彼女はより速く走る / どの女の子よりも / 彼女のクラスの
   She runs _____ / than _____ other _____ /
   in her _____.

2. 言い換えると / 難しい / 不可能ではないとしても / 人々が考えたり行動したりする方法を変えることは / 特に彼らが年を取るにつれて
   In _____ words, / it's hard, / if not _____, /
   to change the way people think and _____, /
   especially _____ they _____.

3. トランペット演奏は / やさしく見える / しかしそれはより難しい / あなたが考えるよりも
   _____ the trumpet / seems _____, /
   but it is _____ difficult / _____ you think.

V Word Order

日本語を参考にして下にある語句を並べ替え英文を完成しなさい。

1. 人々は、しばしば、瞑想の方が薬物治療よりもよりよいと考えます。

   people often / think / better / meditation / medication / that / than / is

   _____

2. これらの実験は、瞑想の効果について示している。

   point to / positive / experiments / the / these / meditation / of / power

   _____

3. 瞑想する人は、瞑想しない人よりも、集中するのがうまい。

   people / concentrate / who / meditate / than / those who / don't / better

   _____

4. 平和な心は、生活の質を向上させるようである。

   a peaceful mind / quality / improves / of / that / life / seems / it

   _____

5. インドでは、ヨガが何世紀も実践されています。

   India, / has / in / centuries / for / been / yoga / practiced

   _____

6. 十分睡眠をとっている人は、ストレスをより感じない傾向がある。

   who / individuals / less / enough / stressed / sleep / to be / tend

   _____

Meditation is good for kids
「瞑想は子どもにもよい！」

最近の研究では、学校での瞑想が子どもによい影響を与えることが示されています。瞑想により、子どもたちの行動が改善され、社交性や自制力が身に付きます。攻撃性が抑えられ、落ち込まなくなり、多動も改善されます。学業成績もよくなりますが、特に集中できるようになるので、数学力がアップします。これらが、瞑想が子どもによいいくつかの理由です。

VI Finding Errors

次の各文には語法または語彙上の誤りが2個所ずつあります。その個所に下線を引き、それを適切な語句に直し（　　）内に記入しなさい。また、全文の日本語訳を書きなさい。

1. People who meditate tends to be less stressed, less anxious and less angrier than those who don't.
   (　　　　　　　　) (　　　　　　　　)

___

2. In Asian countries, meditation was been practiced four centuries.
   (　　　　　　　　) (　　　　　　　　)

___

3. People know that often meditation is good and safe than medication.
   (　　　　　　　　) (　　　　　　　　)

___

4. In order to meditate, they sit comfortably with a strait back, place their hands on their thighs, and low their eyes.
   (　　　　　　　　) (　　　　　　　　)

___

5. But for that who master the technique, it is well worthy the effort.
   (　　　　　　　　) (　　　　　　　　)

___

VII Full Writing

次の日本語を英語に直しなさい。

1. よく知られたことわざは、事実は小説より奇なりということを教えてくれます。

___

2. 高齢の人たちに、新しい外国語を教えることは、不可能とは言えないが、難しいことである。

___

3. ペニシリンの発見のおかげで、新しい治療法が感染症の患者たちのため開発されました。

___

4. 毎日朝食を摂る人の方が、摂らない人よりも集中するのがうまい。

___

Sedona: Harmony with Nature

〈自然の彫刻セドナ〉

CD 57

Once upon a time, the Native American tribes wandered freely across North America. They lived in harmony with nature, but feared its tremendous power. They knew that nature is sometimes as gentle as a soft summer breeze. Other times, it can be as harsh as the cold winter wind.

For the Native Americans, certain places have spiritual power. Red Rock Country, which surrounds the present-day town of Sedona, is a famous example. **If** you visit this area, you will understand why it is special. I did, so now please let me tell you what I learned.

From the hotel terrace, I admired the spectacular red cliffs around Sedona. Over the centuries, the wind, rain and sun have transformed them into magnificent sculptures. One looks like a cathedral, one like a bell and even one like Snoopy resting on his back.

As I gazed in awe at nature's works of art, something mysterious happened. Suddenly I felt that I was part of this beautiful landscape. When I closed my eyes, I was in harmony with myself and the world around me.

My experience is not unusual. For over 100 years, visitors have been coming to Sedona. For different reasons, they want to feel the spiritual energy of this place. Artists and writers seek inspiration for new masterpieces. Individuals suffering from stress hope to unwind through meditation. People with health issues want to try natural, holistic cures. Directors use this dramatic scenery in their films. Tourists come to relax.

If you visit Sedona, you will see and feel the amazing power of nature. It is stronger than all of us, despite our sophisticated technology.

The Native Americans are right. **If** you want to be at peace with yourself, you must live in harmony with nature.

Chapter 12 ◆ Sedona: Harmony with Nature

"MUST-KNOW" collocations and phrases

1. once upon a time 昔々、かつて
2. the Native American tribes アメリカ原住民の部族
3. over the centuries 何世紀の間
4. something mysterious happened 何か不思議なことが起こった
5. close one's eyes 眼を閉じる、瞳を閉じる
6. amazing power of nature 自然の驚くべき力

I Comprehension Questions

本文の内容に合っている文にはTを、合っていない文にはFを（　）内に記入しなさい。

1. (　) For the Native Americans, Red Rock Country has spiritual power.
2. (　) Artists and sculptors have transformed the red cliffs of Sedona into beautiful works of art.
3. (　) For over 100 years, people have been visiting Sedona for many different reasons.

II Guided Summary

次の英文は本文を要約したものです。(1)から(10)の空所に、下の(a)-(j)から適語を選んで記入し文を完成させなさい。

Once upon a time, the Native American tribes (1) _____ freely across North America. They lived in harmony with nature, but feared its (2) _____ power. For the Native Americans, certain places, like the Red Rock Country around Sedona, have (3) _____ power. Over the centuries, the wind, rain and sun have (4) _____ these spectacular red cliffs into magnificent sculptures. When you look at them, you feel part of nature. You are in (5) _____ with yourself and the world around you. For over 100 years, visitors have been coming to Sedona for different (6) _____. Artists and writers seek (7) _____. Stressed individuals want to (8) _____. Sick people try natural (9) _____. Directors make movies. Tourists relax. In Sedona, everybody feels the (10) _____ power of nature. It's important to live in harmony with nature.

[
(a) transformed   (b) inspiration   (c) tremendous   (d) reasons
(e) amazing   (f) harmony   (g) unwind   (h) wandered
(i) cures   (j) spiritual
]

Focus Point 《仮定法現在の if の使い方》

◆ **事実となる可能性が不確かな時の if**

事実となるかならないかの可能性が半々の場合、「If＋主語＋現在形，主節は未来形（または現在形）」の形を使います。主節と if 節の順番を入れ替えることもできます。
If it's sunny, I will go to the beach.（もし晴れたら、私はビーチに行きます）
または、
I will go to the beach **if** it's sunny.（私は、もし晴れたら、ビーチに行きます）
未来形の代わりに may や can を使うこともできます。
If you're free, you can (may) have dinner with me.（もしあなたが暇なら、私と一緒にご飯を食べることができますね）

ex 1) **If** you visit this area, you will understand why it is special.（本文第2段落）

ex 2) **If** you visit Sedona, you will see and feel the amazing power of nature.（本文第6段落）
どちらも似たような if 節ですが、読者が今後その地を訪問することはあるかもしれないし、ないかもしれないので、仮定法現在を使います。

ex 3) **If** you want to be at peace with yourself, you must live in harmony with nature.（本文第7段落）
ここでは if の代わりに when を使うこともできます。

また、この if は命令文とともに使われることもあります。
If the computer is on sale, buy it.（もしそのコンピュータが売りに出されたら、買いなさい）

◆ **確実なことを述べる時の if**

確実なことを言う場合には、「If＋主語＋現在形，現在形の主節」の文型を使います。
If people have no food and water, they die.（もし食物も水もなければ、人は死んでしまいます）
この場合も、if の代わりに when を使うことも可能です。
When people have no food and water, they die.（食物も水もない時、人は死んでしまいます）

◆ **可能性がほとんどないことを仮定する時の if**

「万一〜なら」というように、仮定法現在よりもはるかに不確実な現在および未来についての仮定を表す場合、if 節に should＋原形を使います。ただし、should は本来、助動詞 shall の過去形であるので、これを仮定法過去とみなす場合もあります。
If it should snow in the summer, I would play outside.（万一夏に雪が降れば、私は屋外で遊ぶでしょう）

III Warming up for Writing

（1）次の一連の文字群を、適切に切り離し英文を完成しなさい。ただし〈 〉内の単語が欠落しているので適所に補いなさい。

1. Ifyouthisareayouwillwhyitisspecial. 〈visit, understand〉
   _____

2. AsIgazedaweatnature'sworksofartsomethinghappened. 〈in, mysterious〉
   _____

（2）次の日本語に相当する英語表現になるように（ ）に適語を書きなさい。

1. 自然と調和しながら生きる
   live (　　　) (　　　) (　　　) nature

2. 壮大な彫刻
   (　　　) sculptures

3. 美しい風景
   beautiful (　　　)

4. 様々な理由で
   (　　　) (　　　) reasons

5. この地の精神的エネルギー
   (　　　) energy of this place

6. ストレスに苦しむ人たち
   individuals (　　　) (　　　) stress

7. 健康問題を持つ人々
   people with (　　　) (　　　)

8. 自分自身平和な気持ちになる
   be at (　　　) (　　　) oneself

IV Slash Writing

日本語を見ながら音声を聴き、英文を書き取りなさい。　　CD 59~61

1. 昔々 / アメリカ原住民の部族たちは自由にさまよっていた / 北アメリカを
   Once _____ a _____, /
   the Native American tribes _____ freely / _____ North America.

2. もしあなたがセドナを訪れたら / あなたは見て感じるでしょう / 自然の驚くべき力を
   If you _____ Sedona, / you will _____ and _____ /
   the _____ power of nature.

3. もしあなたがなりたければ / 自分自身平和な気持ちに / あなたは生きなければならない / 自然と調和して
   _____ you want to be / at _____ with yourself, /
   you _____ live / in _____ with nature.

V Word Order

日本語を参考にして下にある語句を並べ替え英文を完成しなさい。

1. そのアメリカ原住民たちは、自然と協調して暮らしていましたが、その強大な力を恐れていました。
   tremendous power / in harmony / its / the Native Americans / feared / with nature, / lived / but

2. そのアメリカ原住民たちは、自然が時に夏のそよ風のように優しいことを知っていました。
   nature is / the Native Americans knew / summer breeze / that / soft / sometimes / as gentle as / a

3. そのアメリカ原住民にとって、ある場所は霊的な力を持っています。
   the / have / power / certain / spiritual / for / places / Native Americans,

4. もしあなたがこの地域を訪れたら、あなたは、なぜそれが特別なのかがわかるでしょう。
   special / will understand / if / why / it is / you visit / this area, / you

5. もしあなたが自然の芸術作品を眺めたら、あなたは突然自分自身がこの美しい風景の一部であると感じるでしょう。
   if / feel / that / you gaze at / you are part of / you will / nature's works of art, / this beautiful landscape

6. もし母親が彼女の赤ちゃんと平和に過ごしたければ、自分自身と調和を持って暮らさなければならない。
   if / wants to be / live in harmony / she must / a mother / with her baby, / at peace / with herself

Grand Canyon
「グランド・キャニオン」

グランド・キャニオンは、セドナから北に車で2時間走ったところにあります。この自然の驚異は、どんな意味から考えても壮大です。長さ（446km）からも幅（最大29km）からも、そして深さ（1800m）においてもです。もしグランド・キャニオンの力を見て感じてみたければ、ヘリコプター・ツアーに参加してみよう。本当にすごいですよ。

VI Finding Errors

次の各文には語法または語彙上の誤りが2個所ずつあります。その個所に下線を引き、それを適切な語句に直し（　）内に記入しなさい。また、全文の日本語訳を書きなさい。

1. Once in a time, the Aborigines wondered freely across the Australian continent.
（　　　　　　　）（　　　　　　　）

2. Japanese people lived in harmonious with nature, but fearful its tremendous power.
（　　　　　　　）（　　　　　　　）

3. Other time, nature can be as harsher as the cold winter wind.
（　　　　　　　）（　　　　　　　）

4. If you wanted to see and feel the power of the Grand Canyon, takes the helicopter tour.
（　　　　　　　）（　　　　　　　）

5. If you were hungry or thirsty, you able open our refrigerator and help yourself to whatever is in it.
（　　　　　　　）（　　　　　　　）

VII Full Writing

次の日本語を英語に直しなさい。

1. 古き日本人たちにとって、ある場所は霊的な力を持っていました。

2. もしあなたが、その学校を訪問すると、なぜそれが特別であるかを理解するでしょう。

3. その男が、その大きな岩を畏怖の念で見つめていると、不思議なことが起こりました。

4. もしあなたが目を閉じれば、あなたはセドナの自然の驚くべき力を感じるでしょう。

Malala: Champion of Education

〈教育のために立ち上がった少女マララ〉

Today people in developed nations believe that every woman, man and child has the right to go to school. Unfortunately in some countries, people are not allowed to study because of gender, race or social status. This discrimination is wrong.

When the Taliban banned education for girls in northern Pakistan, a young teen named Malala refused to obey. She spoke out against this injustice. She also wrote an anonymous blog for the BBC, and described the terrible things that were happening in her country. **If** this outspoken girl **had been** silent, the Taliban **would not have tried** to kill her.

On October 9, 2012, Malala was on the school bus when an armed man suddenly stopped the vehicle. He fired three shots directly at Malala. One bullet hit her in the head. The other two wounded the girls sitting next to her.

Malala's injuries were life-threatening. The doctors decided to fly her to England for intensive treatment. **If** she **had stayed** in Pakistan, she **would have died**.

After a remarkable recovery, Malala continued to be an advocate for education, especially for girls. She has addressed the United Nations on this topic, met world leaders, and received many awards for her courageous work. On October 10, 2014 – exactly two years after the assassination attempt – Malala was co-recipient of the 2014 Nobel Peace Prize. She is the youngest Nobel Laureate ever.

Dictators and extremists fear education because they want to think for us. Education instead gives us the power to think for ourselves. It frees us from ignorance, poverty and prejudice. It teaches us to respect others. That is why Malala wants every child to go to school.

The world **would be** a better and more peaceful place **if** people **listened** to Malala's message about the importance of education.

Chapter 13 ◆ Malala: Champion of Education

"MUST-KNOW" collocations and phrases

1. developed nations　先進国
2. be allowed to ～　～することが許される
3. speak out against ～　～に反対して立ち上がる、～に対して反対意見を述べる
4. the United Nations　国際連合、国連
5. Nobel Peace Prize　ノーベル平和賞
6. respect others　他人を尊重する

I Comprehension Questions

本文の内容に合っている文にはＴを、合っていない文にはＦを（　）内に記入しなさい。

1. (　) Malala spoke out against the Taliban's ban on education for girls.
2. (　) Malala is famous because she won the 2014 Nobel Peace Prize.
3. (　) Dictators want people to be educated so that they can think for themselves.

II Guided Summary

次の英文は本文を要約したものです。(1) から (10) の空所に、下の (a)-(j) から適語を選んで記入し文を完成させなさい。

CD 63

Everybody has the (1) _____ to go to school. Unfortunately some countries do not allow people to study because of (2) _____, race or social status. When the Taliban (3) _____ education for girls in northern Pakistan, a young teen named Malala (4) _____ to obey. As a result, they (5) _____ to kill her. On October 9, 2012, an armed man shot Malala in the head. She was taken to England for intensive (6) _____. If she had stayed in Pakistan, she would have died. After her (7) _____, Malala continued to be an (8) _____ for education, especially for girls. On October 10, 2014, she was co-recipient of the Nobel Peace Prize. Malala knows that education frees us from (9) _____, poverty and prejudice. It also teaches (10) _____ for others.

[
(a) refused　(b) respect　(c) recovery　(d) right　(e) ignorance
(f) treatment　(g) gender　(h) decided　(i) advocate　(j) banned
]

《仮定法過去と仮定法過去完了の if の使い方》

◆ **現在の事実に反することを仮定する時の if（仮定法過去）**

現在の事実に反することを仮定する場合は、過去形を用いた仮定法を使います。それを仮定法過去と呼びます。

If I were[was] a bird, I **would fly** to you.（もし私が鳥だったら、あなたのところに飛んで行くだろう）

仮定法過去の有名な例文。「私が鳥だったら」と現在の事実に反することを仮定しているので過去形 were[was] が使われています。仮定法では、主語に関わらず be 動詞を were にするのが伝統的でしたが、現在では、主語が一人称（I）、三人称（he, she など）の時はしばしば was も用いられます。

ex 1) The world **would be** a better and more peaceful place **if** people **listened** to Malala's message about the importance of education.（本文第 7 段落）

if 節の動詞が listened と過去形になっている仮定法過去の文。「人々がマララのメッセージに耳を傾けたら」と現在の事実に反することを仮定しています。

◆ **過去の事実に反することを仮定する時の if（仮定法過去完了）**

過去の事実に反することを仮定する場合は、仮定法過去完了を用いて表します。

If we **had gone** out in the storm then, we **would not be** living now.（もしあの時嵐の中を出かけていたら、私たちは今、生きていなかっただろう）

ex 2) **If** this outspoken girl **had been** silent, the Taliban **would not have tried** to kill her.（本文第 2 段落）

「もし黙っていたなら」という意味であり、実際には黙っていなかった → 過去の事実に反する

ex 3) **If** she **had stayed** in Pakistan, she **would have died**.（本文第 4 段落）

「もしパキスタンにとどまっていたら」という意味であり、実際にはとどまっていなかった → 過去の事実に反する

◆ **その他の仮定法**

if it were not for ~ で「~がなければ」、if it had not been for ~ で「~がなかったならば」の意味を表します。

If it were not for water, everybody would die.（もし水がなければ、皆死ぬだろう）
If it had not been for his home run, our team would have lost the game.（もし彼のホームランがなかったならば、私たちのチームは試合に負けていただろう）

III Warming up for Writing

(1) 次の一連の文字群を、適切に切り離し英文を完成しなさい。ただし〈　〉内の単語が欠落しているので適所に補いなさい。

1. IfshestayedinPakistanshewoulddied. 〈had, have〉

_____

2. Dictatorsandextremistseducationbecausetheywanttothinkus. 〈fear, for〉

_____

(2) 次の日本語に相当する英語表現になるように (　) に適語を書きなさい。

1. 勉強をすることが許されない
   not be (　　　) (　　　) study

2. 従うことを拒否する
   (　　　) to obey

3. 彼女の頭に命中する
   hit her (　　　) (　　　) (　　　)

4. 史上最年少ノーベル賞受賞者
   the (　　　) Nobel (　　　) ever

5. 独裁者や過激論者
   (　　　) and (　　　)

6. 自分たち自身のために考える力
   the (　　　) to think (　　　) ourselves

7. だから
   that is (　　　)

8. 教育の大切さ
   the (　　　) of (　　　)

IV Slash Writing

日本語を見ながら音声を聴き、英文を書き取りなさい。　　🎧 CD 64~66

1. 不幸なことにいくつかの国々では / 人々が勉強をすることを許されていません / 性別のため / 人種や社会的地位

   Unfortunately in _____ countries, / people are not _____ to study / because of _____, / _____ or social _____.

2. もしこの歯に衣着せぬ少女が / 黙っていたとしたら / タリバンはしようとしなかったであろう / 彼女を殺すことを

   If this _____ girl / _____ been silent, / the Taliban would not _____ _____ / to _____ her.

3. 世界はなっているだろう / よりよく、そしてより平和な場所に / もし人々がマララのメッセージに耳を傾けていたならば / 教育の重要性についての

   The world _____ be / a better and _____ peaceful place / if people _____ to Malala's message / about the _____ of education.

V Word Order

日本語を参考にして下にある語句を並べ替え英文を完成しなさい。

1. もし彼女がこの権利の侵害に対して声を上げなかったら、タリバンは彼女を殺そうとしなかったであろう。
   to kill her / the Taliban / she had not / would not / against this injustice, / if / spoken out / have tried

___

2. もしその少女たちがマララの隣に座っていなかったら、彼女たちは負傷しなかっただろう。
   would not have / had not been / been wounded / if / they / the girls / sitting / next to Malala,

___

3. 医師たちは、集中治療のため彼女をイングランドに飛行機で移送することを決めました。
   England / fly / to / for / her / decided to / the doctors / intensive treatment

___

4. 教育は、その代わり、私たちに自分たちのために考える力を与えます。
   education / for ourselves / us / think / gives / instead / to / the power

___

5. 教育は、人々を無知や貧困や偏見から解放します。
   people / prejudice / and / poverty / education / ignorance, / from / frees

___

6. もし私がもう10歳若かったら、英語の勉強をしっかりするのに。
   I / were / if / very hard / ten years younger, / I / study English / would

___

The DOVE is a symbol of peace
「ハトは平和のシンボル」

ハトはとても特別な鳥です。ハトの夫婦は、生涯連れ添い、協働してヒナのために巣作りをします。多くの文化で、ハトが平和のシンボルになっていることは当然のことです。時に、ハトはオリーブの枝をくちばしにくわえて運びます。平和を求める人は、しばしば、ハト派と呼ばれます。

Chapter 13 ◆ Malala: Champion of Education

VI Finding Errors

次の各文には語法または語彙上の誤りが2個所ずつあります。その個所に下線を引き、それを適切な語句に直し(　)内に記入しなさい。また、全文の日本語訳を書きなさい。

1. Most people in Japan believe that every women, man and child has the left to go to school.
　　　　　　　　　　　　　　　　(　　　　　　) (　　　　　　)
_____

2. Unfortunately in some nations, people are not allow to study because of gender, racing or social status.
　　　　　　　　　　　　　　　　(　　　　　　) (　　　　　　)
_____

3. If Malala had not written an unanimous blog for the BBC, she would not have been wound.
　　　　　　　　　　　　　　　　(　　　　　　) (　　　　　　)
_____

4. One day, she was on the school bus when an armless man saddened stopped the vehicle.
　　　　　　　　　　　　　　　　(　　　　　　) (　　　　　　)
_____

5. If the bullet had not hitted her by the head, the doctors would not have sent her to England.
　　　　　　　　　　　　　　　　(　　　　　　) (　　　　　　)
_____

VII Full Writing

次の日本語を英語に直しなさい。

1. もし彼らが家にとどまっていたら、彼らは誘拐されることはなかったであろう。
_____

2. 不幸なことに、当時の日本では、女性が投票することは許されていませんでした。
_____

3. 彼らは、その傷ついたハトを動物病院に連れて行くことを決めた。
_____

4. もし、彼がトルコにとどまっていたら、彼は殺されることはなかったであろう。
_____

Universities: Past, Present and Future

〈大学の移り変わり〉

The word "university" was originally used in Italy to describe a community of scholars and students. The University of Bologna, **founded in 1088**, was the first of its kind in Europe. Other European cities were quick to follow Bologna's example: the University of Paris (1096), the English universities of Oxford (around 1096) and Cambridge (1204), and the University of Salamanca (Spain – 1218). Since then, universities have been founded all over the world.

Although more than 900 years have passed, the teaching model has not changed very much – large lectures, small seminars, and laboratory practice. Today, **however**, this traditional system is under attack. Students and their families often are forced to take out big loans because the cost of higher education, **especially in the US**, has skyrocketed. Professors have little or no interaction with their students because their classes are overcrowded.

Recently some colleges and universities have been offering online courses to replace traditional lectures. This system has certain advantages. First, it allows students to study at their own pace and to review difficult or confusing sections. Second, online courses are less expensive than lectures. Critics, **however**, insist that online learning cannot replace the classroom experience.

For now, the university of the future will probably be a "blended model" – that is, the traditional system of lectures, seminars and labs combined with online courses. This system helps both the university administration and the students. These courses save money for the university. They also encourage enrollment, **especially among non-traditional students**, because online courses offer greater flexibility in scheduling. When enrollment increases, the university has more money to defray expenses.

Whatever the university of the future will be, this institution is important. Education gives us the power to make positive changes in ourselves and in society.

Chapter 14 ◆ Universities: Past, Present and Future

"MUST-KNOW" collocations and phrases

1. the first of its kind その種のものの最初
2. not ~ very much あまり~ない
3. be under attack 攻撃を受けている、危機に陥っている
4. be forced to ~ ~せざるを得ない
5. higher education 高等教育
6. have little or no ~ ~がほとんどあるいは全くない

I Comprehension Questions

本文の内容に合っている文にはTを、合っていない文にはFを（　）内に記入しなさい。

1. (　) The University of Bologna was the first European university.
2. (　) Today everybody agrees that the traditional teaching models should include online courses.
3. (　) Online courses save money for the university, increase enrollment, and give students greater flexibility in scheduling.

II Guided Summary

次の英文は本文を要約したものです。(1) から (10) の空所に、下の (a)-(j) から適語を選んで記入し文を完成させなさい。　🎧 68

The University of Bologna, (1) _____ in 1088, is the oldest in Europe. Other European cities soon (2) _____ Bologna's example, and formed new universities. Although more than 900 years have passed, the (3) _____ teaching model in universities has not changed very much. Today this system is under (4) _____. The cost of higher education, especially in the US, has (5) _____. Professors have little or no (6) _____ with their students because classes are overcrowded. Universities are now offering online courses to (7) _____ lectures. Because these courses are less expensive, they help defray expenses. Despite (8) _____ from critics, the university of the future will probably use a (9) "_____ model" – traditional and online courses. Education is important because it gives us the power to make (10) _____ change.

[
(a) attack　　(b) interaction　　(c) positive　　(d) replace
(e) followed　(f) opposition　　(g) blended　　(h) founded
(i) traditional　(j) skyrocketed
]

Focus Point 《挿入句の使い方》

文構造が簡単で一文一文が短い文章は、単調で面白みに欠けます。英語を書く際には挿入句をうまく使うと趣のある文章となります。

◆ 主節が挿入句になる場合

「主語＋動詞」という形が挿入句として用いられる場合は、それが文の主節である場合が多くなります。

The student who was singing on the stage, **I thought,** would surely be a professional singer in the future.（ステージで歌っている学生は、将来確実にプロの歌手になるのではと私は思いました）
この文は、I thought that the student who was singing on the stage would be a professional singer in the future. と書き変えることが可能。

◆ 従属節が挿入句になる場合

文の途中に挿入される従属節は、通常、副詞句になります。

My son's routine work in summer, **when it is not raining**, is to water the plants in the garden.
（雨が降っていない時、庭の植物の水やりは息子の夏の仕事です）

◆ 形容詞句・副詞句が挿入句になる場合

形容詞句や副詞句の前後をコンマで囲い、修飾語句として文に挿入します。

ex 1) The University of Bologna, **founded in 1088,** was the first of its kind in Europe.（本文第1段落）
founded in 1088（1088年に創立された）は、The University of Bologna を修飾する形容詞句です。

ex 2) Students and their families often are forced to take out big loans because the cost of higher education, **especially in the US,** has skyrocketed.（本文第2段落）
especially in the US（特に合衆国においては）を強調するために挿入句として書かれています。

ex 3) They also encourage enrollment, **especially among non-traditional students,** because online courses offer greater flexibility in scheduling.（本文第4段落）
especially among non-traditional students（特にこれまでとは違う種類の学生たちにおいては）という副詞句を強調的に挿入句として用います。

◆ 接続詞としての however

however は文頭に置くこともありますが、挿入句として文中に置くと、より洗練された文になります。

ex 4) Today, **however**, this traditional system is under attack.（本文第2段落）
ex 5) Critics, **however**, insist that online learning cannot replace the classroom experience.（本文第3段落）

Chapter 14 ◆ Universities: Past, Present and Future

III Warming up for Writing

（1）次の一連の文字群を、適切に切り離し英文を完成しなさい。ただし〈　〉内の単語が欠落しているので適所に補いなさい。

1. TheUniversityofBolognafoundedin1088wasthefirstkindinEurope.〈of, its〉
_____

2. Professorshaveorinteractionwiththeirstudentsbecausetheirclassesareovercrowded.
〈little, no〉
_____

（2）次の日本語に相当する英語表現になるように（　）に適語を書きなさい。

1. もともと使われている
　 be (　　　　) used
2. 学者と学生の共同体
　 a (　　　　) of (　　　　) and students
3. 急いで〜に続く
　 be (　　　　) to follow 〜
4. それ以来
　 (　　　　) then
5. 多額のローンを組む
　 (　　　　)(　　　　) big loans
6. オンラインコース
　 (　　　　) courses
7. 〜に…させる
　 (　　　　) 〜 to …
8. 〜自身のペースで
　 at one's (　　　　) pace

IV Slash Writing

日本語を見ながら音声を聴き、英文を書き取りなさい。　🎧 69~71

1. 学生とその家族は / しばしば多額のローンを組むことを余儀なくされる / なぜならば高等教育の経費が / 特にアメリカ合衆国の場合は / 高騰しているからです
　 Students and their _____ /
　 often are forced to _____ out big loans /
　 because the cost of higher _____, / _____ in the US, /
　 has _____.

2. 教授は、ほとんどあるいは全く関わりがありません / 彼らの学生たちと / なぜなら彼らの授業は人数が多すぎるからです
　 Professors have _____ or no interaction / with their _____ /
　 because their classes are _____.

3. 批評家たちはしかしながら / 主張します / オンライン学習はとってかわることはできないと / 教室での経験に
　 Critics, _____, / _____ that /
　 online learning cannot _____ / the classroom _____.

87

V Word Order

日本語を参考にして下にある語句を並べ替え英文を完成しなさい。

1. ヨーロッパの他の都市たちは、もちろん、ボローニャの例に急いで続きました。
   follow / other / to / of course, / quick / Bologna's example / European cities, / were

2. 今日では、しかしながら、この伝統的なシステムが危機に陥っています。
   system / traditional / under / today, / attack / is / this / however,

3. 高等教育の費用が、特に米国で、高騰してしまった。
   higher education, / the cost / has / of / the US, / in / especially / skyrocketed

4. 第二に、オンラインコースは、講義よりも費用が安い。
   second, / lectures / courses / are / than / online / expensive / less

5. このシステムは、大学当局にとっても学生たちにとっても、双方の役に立ちます。
   helps / both / and / this system / the / university / administration / the students

6. 入学者が増えれば、大学は費用を支払うお金が増えます。
   expenses / when / to defray / the university / more money / increases, / has / enrollment

The Oldest University in the World
「世界最古の大学」

モロッコのフェズにあるアル・カラウィン大学は、世界最古の大学です。その大学は、西暦859年に裕福なファティマ・アル－フィーリという未亡人によって設立されました。彼女は、遺産をこの事業に費やしました。世界記録のギネスブックによると、その大学は西暦859年から学位を絶え間なく出し続けているとのことです。

VI Finding Errors

次の各文には語法または語彙上の誤りが2個所ずつあります。その個所に下線を引き、それを適切な語句に直し（　）内に記入しなさい。また、全文の日本語訳を書きなさい。

1. Since them, ballparks have been fund all over Japan.
   (　　　　　　　) (　　　　　　　)

2. Although more than 900 years has passed, the festival has not changed very little.
   (　　　　　　　) (　　　　　　　)

3. College students and their families, especially in the US, often are forcing to take away big loans.
   (　　　　　　　) (　　　　　　　)

4. Recently some colleges and universities have been offered online courses to replace traditionally lectures.
   (　　　　　　　) (　　　　　　　)

5. They also encourage enrollment, especial among non-traditional students, because online courses offer greater flexible in scheduling.
   (　　　　　　　) (　　　　　　　)

VII Full Writing

次の日本語を英語に直しなさい。

1. 1877年以来、その年に東京大学が設立されたのであるが、大学は日本中に設立されてきている。

2. 土地と住宅の値段が高騰しているので、特に都市部においては、多くの日本人は多額のローンを組むことを余儀なくさせられる。

3. その大学当局の職員は、学生たちとはほとんどあるいは全く関わりを持たない。

4. 教育は私たちに世界をよりよく、より平和な場所にする力を与えてくれます。

Lighting up the Future

〈未来を照らす〉

People have always been afraid of the dark. About half a million years ago, our ancestors began to conquer this fear when they learned to create light from fire. Since then, people have been inventing new ways to get more light by using candles, and oil or gas lamps. Unfortunately these methods were often dangerous fire hazards.

When and where did someone find a better solution? In 1879, Thomas Alva Edison, an American inventor and businessman, made the first practical electric light bulb in New Jersey. It was a safer way to produce light.

In the 1960's, scientists wanted to find a substitute for traditional light bulbs. Their goal was to create white light by combining red, green and blue light-emitting diodes (LEDs). Red and green LEDs already existed. The challenge was a blue LED. If they solved that problem, they would change lighting technology.

Who succeeded? In 1989, three Japanese scientists – Dr. Isamu Akasaki, Dr. Hiroshi Amano and Prof. Shuji Nakamura – created blue light. Although it took years of trial and error, they had the dedication, patience and work ethic to follow their dream.

Their discovery is revolutionizing the 21st century. The LED technology offers a better way to light up our lives. How is this possible?

LED bulbs are more efficient than traditional ones because they last longer, consume less energy, and produce less heat. They are safer for our health. They are also environmentally-friendly because, unlike fluorescent lights, they don't contain mercury. That is why these three Japanese scientists won the 2014 Nobel Prize for physics.

What can we learn from Akasaki, Amano and Nakamura? Like them, we should believe in our dreams. We must never give up. If we follow their example, we will make the future brighter.

Chapter 15 ◆ Lighting up the Future

"MUST-KNOW" collocations and phrases

1. dangerous fire hazard(s) 危険な火事の原因となりうるもの
2. practical electric light bulb 実用的な電球
3. light-emitting diode(s) 発光ダイオード（LED）
4. trial and error 試行錯誤
5. fluorescent light 蛍光灯
6. Nobel Prize for physics ノーベル物理学賞

I Comprehension Questions

本文の内容に合っている文にはTを、合っていない文にはFを（　）内に記入しなさい。

1. (　) Thomas Alva Edison's electric light bulb was safer than candles, and oil or gas lamps.
2. (　) Three Japanese scientists spent many years trying to create green and red LEDs.
3. (　) LED bulbs last longer, consume less energy, and produce more heat than traditional bulbs.

II Guided Summary

次の英文は本文を要約したものです。(1)から(10)の空所に、下の(a)-(j)から適語を選んで記入し文を完成させなさい。

People have always been afraid of the dark. About half a million years ago, our (1) _____ learned to use fire as a (2) _____ of light. Since then, people have been (3) _____ new ways to create light. In 1879, Thomas Alva Edison made the first (4) _____ electric light bulb. In the 1960's, scientists wanted to create white light by (5) _____ red, green and blue light-emitting diodes. The (6) _____ was a blue LED. In 1989, three Japanese scientists – Dr. Isamu Akasaki, Dr. Hiroshi Amano and Prof. Shuji Nakamura – succeeded. LED bulbs last longer, (7) _____ less energy, (8) _____ less heat, and are safer for our health and the environment. That is why these three Japanese (9) _____ won the 2014 Nobel Prize for physics. Like them, we must (10) _____ in our dreams and never give up.

(a) practical　(b) scientists　(c) challenge　(d) ancestors　(e) believe
(f) consume　(g) produce　(h) source　(i) combining　(j) inventing

Focus Point 《まとめ》

Chapter 15 の文章には、Chapter 1～Chapter 14 までの Focus Point の文法内容が含まれています。本文の中から、次の各ポイントを探し、下線を引きチャプター番号を記してみましょう。

Chapter 1: why の使い方
- 理由を尋ねる why（疑問詞の why） ◆ 理由を修飾する why（関係副詞の why）
- その他の why を用いた表現

Chapter 2: who/whom の使い方
- 「誰か」を尋ねる who（疑問詞の who） ◆ 「どんな人なのか」を説明する who（関係代名詞の who）
- 「誰に」を尋ねる whom（疑問詞の whom）

Chapter 3: when の使い方
- 時を尋ねる when（疑問詞の when） ◆ 「～した（する）時に」を表す when（接続詞の when）
- 時を説明する when（関係副詞の when）

Chapter 4: how の使い方
- 方法を尋ねる how（疑問詞の how） ◆ 「how＋to 不定詞」
- 感嘆文を作る how（感嘆詞の how） ◆ 程度を尋ねる how

Chapter 5: where の使い方
- 場所を尋ねる where（疑問詞の where） ◆ 場所を説明する where（関係副詞の where）
- その他の where の用法

Chapter 6: what の使い方
- 「何」であるかを尋ねる what（疑問詞の what）
- 「～すること（もの）」を表す what（関係代名詞詞の what） ◆ その他の what を用いた表現

Chapter 7: 助動詞の使い方
- would ◆ may ◆ must ◆ can ◆ should

Chapter 8: 動名詞と現在分詞の使い方
- 動名詞 ◆ 現在分詞

Chapter 9: 現在完了形と現在完了進行形の使い方
- 現在完了 ◆ 現在完了進行形

Chapter 10: 接続詞の使い方
- 時を示す接続詞 ◆ 原因・理由を示す接続詞 ◆ 目的を示す接続詞 ◆ 譲歩を示す接続詞

Chapter 11: 比較級の使い方
- 形容詞の語尾に -er をつける場合 ◆ 形容詞の前に more をつける場合 ◆ 不規則変化の場合
- less をつける劣等比較の場合

Chapter 12: 仮定法現在の if の使い方
- 事実となる可能性が不確かな時の if ◆ 確実なことを述べる時の if
- 可能性がほとんどないことを仮定する時の if

Chapter 13: 仮定法過去と仮定法過去完了の if の使い方
- 現在の事実に反することを仮定する時の if（仮定法過去）
- 過去の事実に反することを仮定する時の if（仮定法過去完了） ◆ その他の仮定法

Chapter 14: 挿入句の使い方
- 主節が挿入句になる場合 ◆ 従属節が挿入句になる場合
- 形容詞句・副詞句が挿入句になる場合 ◆ 接続詞としての however

Chapter 15　Lighting up the Future

III Warming up for Writing

（1）次の一連の文字群を、適切に切り離し英文を完成しなさい。ただし〈　〉内の単語が欠落しているので適所に補いなさい。

1. Peoplehavealwaysafraidthedark.〈been, of〉

_____

2. Ifwetheirexamplewewillmakethefuture.〈follow, brighter〉

_____

（2）次の日本語に相当する英語表現になるように（　）に適語を書きなさい。

1. 闇をおそれる
　be afraid of (　　　)(　　　)

2. 約50万年前
　about (　　　) a (　　　) years ago

3. 光を生み出すためのより安全な方法
　a (　　　) way to (　　　) light

4. 従来の電球
　(　　　) light bulbs

5. より長持ちする
　(　　　) longer

6. より少ないエネルギーを消費する
　(　　　) less (　　　)

7. 熱の発生が少ない
　(　　　) less heat

8. 水銀を含む
　contain (　　　)

IV Slash Writing

日本語を見ながら音声を聴き、英文を書き取りなさい。　　　CD 74〜76

1. それ以来 / 人々は新しい方法をずっと考案してきました / より多くの光を得る / ろうそくを使って / あるいは油またはガスのランプで

　_____ then, / people have been inventing new _____ /
　to _____ more light / by using _____ , /
　and oil or gas _____ .

2. 1879年に / トーマス・アルバ・エジソン / アメリカの発明家であり実業家でもあるが / 最初の実用的電球を作り出しました / ニュージャージー州で

　_____ 1879, / Thomas Alva Edison, /
　an American _____ and businessman, /
　made the first _____ electric light bulb / in New Jersey.

3. 1960年代 / 科学者たちは見つけたいと思っていた / 従来の電球の代わりになるものを

　In the _____ , / _____ wanted to find /
　a _____ for traditional light bulbs.

V Word Order

日本語を参考にして下にある語句を並べ替え英文を完成しなさい。

1. 人間は、常に闇が怖いと思っています。

   people / been / always / have / of / dark / afraid / the

   _____

2. 不幸なことに、これらの方法はしばしば、危険な火事の原因となるものであった。

   these / were / dangerous / often / hazards / unfortunately / fire / methods

   _____

3. もし、その問題を解決したら、彼らは光学技術を変えることになるだろう。

   lighting technology / solved / would / if / change / they / they / that problem,

   _____

4. LED の技術は私たちの生活を照らすよりよい方法を提供します。

   lives / our / a better way / offers / up / light /the LED technology / to

   _____

5. だから、これら3人の日本人科学者たちが2014年のノーベル物理学賞を獲得したのです。

   is / why / that / for physics / these / three Japanese scientists / the 2014 Nobel Prize / won

   _____

6. もし私たちが彼らの例に従えば、私たちは未来を明るくするでしょう。

   follow / the future / will make / brighter / if / we / we / their example,

   _____

Controlling Daylight
「昼の光を制御する」

多くの国々、特に西洋諸国では、デイライト・セイビング・タイム（DST，夏時間）を採用しています。一般的に3月初めから11月の初めまで、時計が1時間進められます。DSTを採用すると、夕方の明るい時間が長くなります。だから人々は学校や仕事が終わった後、外で楽しむことができます。あなたは、DSTはいい考えだと思いますか。

VI Finding Errors

次の各文には語法または語彙上の誤りが2個所ずつあります。その個所に下線を引き、それを適切な語句に直し（　　）内に記入しなさい。また、全文の日本語訳を書きなさい。

1. About five hundred thousand years ago, our ancestors begun to conquer this fear which they learned to create light from fire.
(　　　　　　　) (　　　　　　　)

2. Science then, people have been inventing new ways to get many light by using candles, and oil or gas lamps.
(　　　　　　　) (　　　　　　　)

3. In 1879, Thomas Alva Edison, an American inventor and businessman, made the first practical electric right bulb in New Jersey.
(　　　　　　　) (　　　　　　　)

4. The discovery is revolutionary the 21th century.
(　　　　　　　) (　　　　　　　)

5. That is the reason these three Japanese scientists winning the 2014 Nobel Prize for physicians.
(　　　　　　　) (　　　　　　　)

VII Full Writing

次の日本語を英語に直しなさい。

1. 人々はいつでも地震をおそれてきました。

2. 従来の蛍光灯をLED電球に変えることは、環境に優しいと同時に財布にも優しい。

3. それが、若いパキスタンの少女が2014年のノーベル平和賞を受賞した理由です。

4. もしあなたがこの教科書を使って英語を勉強したら、あなたは未来をより明るくするでしょう。

TEXT PRODUCTION STAFF

edited by　　　編集
Takashi Kudo　　工藤 隆志

cover design by　　表紙デザイン
Ruben Frosali　　ルーベン・フロサリ

illustrated by　　イラスト
Yoko Sekine　　関根 庸子

CD PRODUCTION STAFF

narrated by　　吹き込み者
Chris Koprowski (AmE)　　クリス・コプロスキ（アメリカ英語）
Rachel Walzer (AmE)　　レイチェル・ワルザー（アメリカ英語）

Read Well, Write Better
リーディングで鍛える英作文

2016年1月20日　初版　発行
2024年2月10日　第12刷　発行

著　者　　Joan McConnell
　　　　　武田 修一
　　　　　山内 圭
発行者　　佐野 英一郎
発行所　　株式会社 成美堂
　　　　　〒101-0052　東京都千代田区神田小川町3-22
　　　　　TEL 03-3291-2261　FAX 03-3293-5490
　　　　　https://www.seibido.co.jp

印刷・製本　倉敷印刷(株)

ISBN 978-4-7919-4787-4　　　　　　　　　　Printed in Japan

・落丁・乱丁本はお取り替えします。
・本書の無断複写は、著作権上の例外を除き著作権侵害となります。